if you 're

clueless

about

the

stock

market

and

want to

know more

if you 're

clueless

about

the

stock

market

2nd Edition

and

want to

know more

by SETH GODIN

DEARBORN™
T R A D E
A **Kaplan Professional** Company

If You're Clueless about the Stock Market and Want to Know More

This publication is designed to provide accurate and authoritative information in regard to the subject matter covered. It is sold with the understanding that the publisher is not engaged in rendering legal, accounting, or other professional service. If legal advice or other expert assistance is required, the services of a competent professional person should be sought.

Publisher: Cynthia A. Zigmund
Managing Editor: Jack Kiburz
Project Editor: Trey Thoelcke
Interior and Cover Design: Karen Englemann

© 1997, 2001 by Seth Godin Productions, Inc.

Published by Dearborn Trade, a Kaplan Professional Company

All rights reserved. The text of this publication, or any part thereof, may not be reproduced in any manner whatsoever without written permission from the publisher.

Printed in the United States of America

01 02 03 10 9 8 7 6 5 4 3 2 1

Library of Congress Cataloging-in-Publication Data
Godin, Seth.
    If you're clueless about the stock market and want to know more /
Seth Godin.— 2nd ed.
        p.   cm.
    Includes index.
    ISBN 0-7931-4367-5 (pbk.)
    1. Stocks—United States.   2. Investments—United States.   3. Stock
exchanges—United States.   I. Title.
HG4910 .G59 2001
332.63'22—dc21

00-012909

Dearborn Trade books are available at special quantity discounts to use as premiums and sales promotions, or for use in corporate training programs. For more information, please call the Special Sales Manager at 800-621-9621, ext. 4514, or write to Dearborn Financial Publishing, Inc., 155 North Wacker Drive, Chicago, IL 60606-1719.

Acknowledgments

Thanks to Jack Kiburz and Cindy Zigmund at Dearborn, whose editorial guidance made this book possible. Karen Watts was the driving force behind the Clueless concept, and Ed Aviza did an expert job of pulling it all together.

Thanks to Robin Dellabough, Lisa DiMona, Nana Sledzieski, Leslie Sharp, Susan Kushnick, Lisa Lindsay, Julie Maner, and Sarah Silbert at SGP for their legendary insight and hard work. And finally thanks to Rachel Hoyt and Lindsay Stowe for their efforts to keep this book in the present tense.

Contents

GETTING *a clue* about the *stock* MARKET

CHAPTER ONE

By *buying stocks, you're buying a piece of corporate America. You become an* **owner**—*someone vilified by Marx and glorified by the American forefathers, who can now expect random phone calls over dinner as yet another broker tries to sell you the next* **hot stock.**

You're hip, you're educated. You think you're pretty sharp. You read. You watch the news. You listen to the radio. They mention the stock market, and your eyes glaze over.

You've heard about the phenomenal success and wealth the stock market can create—maybe you've even seen your friends make profits while you've been waiting cautiously. Right now it may seem too complicated, risky, and even a little scary—you've heard that fortunes can be made fast and then lost just as quickly.

The fact is that the stock market can be tremendously effective in helping you achieve your financial goals. Despite all those frightening things you've heard about "crashes"

and "bulls" and "bears," careful, considered investing in the stock market can yield a lifetime of financial security.

Are you ready to find out how to join the millions of people who have overcome their fears of the unknown to plunge into the exciting world of the stock market? Strap on your safety belt! You're going to learn how to become an investor.

Be Careful Out There!

While plenty of reasons exist to be optimistic about the long-term financial benefits of investing in stocks, individual investors need to temper optimism with a solid dose of caution and good sense. Stocks can be very lucrative investments, but they can easily be as slippery as fish if you aren't careful about what you pick up. Stocks tend to be more volatile in the short term than many other investments, so you'll need to have a strong stomach and a willingness to endure uncertainty.

You may have to watch the value of your investments rise and fall like a roller coaster. No straight line runs from the bottom of the pile to the top of the heap. Stock charts show how stock prices climb and fall in a pattern of spikes and curves that makes California's coastal highways look as straight as the endless roads of Death Valley. The keys to success here are patience, a long-term perspective, and knowledge about what you are putting your money into.

Think Long Term

Exactly what is a long-term versus a short-term perspective? Stocks react to changes in fortune continuously. If you take a short-term outlook, you react continuously too. The long-term perspective is measured in years, not in hours, days, or even weeks. If you base your buy and sell decisions on frequently updated reports without taking the longer-term outlook of the company into account, you will most likely not be a tremendous success in the stock market.

Why not jump right out of a stock if the company has a bad first quarter? Because the second quarter might be great, and the third quarter may be good as well. Of course, the fourth quarter may not be so terrific. The point is that no one can accurately predict the future. Bouncing in and out of stocks on the basis of short-term conditions implies that you know the long-term effect these short-term conditions will have on the stock, something that is really difficult to know. And not knowing the future means that, more often than not, the timing of your transactions will be wrong and cause you regret.

To consider the long-term potential of a stock means that you take into account dozens of factors that can predictably affect the fortunes of a company over the long haul, and even these factors can't be 100 percent accurate in every case. This book will give you a primer on some of the many things to consider when looking at stocks to sink your earnings into.

To further complicate matters, no company exists in a vacuum. If you think the Wacky Widgee Company is going to have a great year because the latest fashion fad is widgees, but you neglect to take into account the broader economic conditions of the country (or the world), you may be in for a rude awakening. Suppose that those wacky widgees are what is known as "luxury" or "impulse" items; most people only wear them as fun accessories, not as necessities (like coats in a freezing climate, for example). If a large number of people have good, stable jobs and a surplus of disposable income, your widgee maker's latest fad may drive its stock through the roof. But if the rest of the economy is struggling through a recession and the amount of discretionary income people have for fun stuff like widgees is at an all-time low, you may find yourself holding onto worthless shares of another victim of the general economic malaise.

Automobile stocks work this way, too. If the economy is in a general recession and, to add insult to injury, the price of gasoline has soared into the stratosphere, you can pretty much expect that auto company stocks will decline.

Be Aware

It pays to know what's going on in the world. Being able to recognize certain market conditions enables you to make informed choices about where to invest your money— not only for growth, but also for safety.

The way to keep up-to-date is to read. Read the newspapers, particularly the business sections, for economic and corporate news that could affect your investments. *The*

Wall Street Journal and *Barron's* are particularly helpful. Read financial, political, and news magazines like *Kiplinger's, Forbes, Fortune, Money, Time,* and *Newsweek.*

If you're looking for a great way to stay informed, get online. You can find exactly what you're looking for from a thousand different sources by connecting to the Internet and searching for topics that interest you. If you want to keep up with happenings that directly affect Wacky Widgees, you can join electronic mailing lists and newsgroups that will keep you abreast of moment-by-moment changes in the company's fortunes. You can also easily obtain pertinent information such as whether Wally's Widgees (Wacky's biggest competitor) has produced an even cooler widgee that may all but freeze the sales of your company's products and send that stock of yours straight down the proverbial toilet. (See the Resources section on page 201 for a list of some of the most helpful online sources.)

Never Fall in Love with a Stock

No matter how much you've earned from a stock, you can always lose money, too. Sometimes losses turn to gains rapidly and although lots of advisors and investment analysts are all ready to offer opinions, you really have to decide for yourself when it is appropriate to buy or sell. If you've experienced a heavy "paper loss" on a particular stock (a loss that you haven't actually realized by selling the stock), you may just want to bite the bullet, sell, and move into a better position by reinvesting the money elsewhere.

On the other hand, if the company is still in good shape and you think the current low price is an aberration, you may want to "average down" your investment costs on the stock by buying more at the lower price. You have to do your research and stay on top of the company that you're invested in. If the price turns for the worse, consider selling regardless of how much that stock has earned for you. If you're reluctant to sell, try to find out why the stock's value has dropped and whether the company is still a good bet for the long term.

Hanging on to a continuously dropping stock may be bad not only for your pocketbook but also for your digestion and your ability to sleep at night. And if you've experienced a decent "paper gain," it may behoove you to sell and lock in some profits while you still have the chance. While it's impossible to forecast the future with complete accuracy, if you read on you'll learn a few things to watch for that will help you

make your decisions. A key point to remember in all of this is that you have to be the master of your own emotions. Don't let greed or fear get in the way of a solid, rational approach to managing your investments.

Why Invest in the Stock Market?

The basic function of the stock market is to provide capital resources for corporations that seek to expand their operations and finance their growth. If you make your money available to these companies, you help them expand and prosper. At the same time, you have the chance to make a profit on your investment. But much more is going on than individuals simply trying to make a buck. The stock market encompasses a whole range of economic and social structures that are an integral part of the economic foundation of the United States, and the world. Individual investors seeking to earn profitable returns on their investments participate in this market alongside enormous (and not so enormous) corporations that seek to find funding for their projects and operations.

Mutual funds provide individuals with greater exposure to diverse sets of investments than they could provide for themselves. Funds also create jobs for thousands of people working in the financial industries. Banks that house the savings of millions of citizens invest in stocks and mutual funds in order to profitably hedge against the ravages of inflation. Stocks and stock-related investments enable insurance companies to finance continuing operations and produce sources of capital to fund the payment of claims and the expansion of business. Pension and retirement funds use investments to maximize returns and attempt to provide financial security and stability for the retirement years of their members. The prices of groups of stocks are gathered together in "indexes" that provide measuring tools to gauge the general health of the economy. By investing in the stock market, you are directly participating in the great engine that drives the nation's economy and determines its prosperity and health.

STOCK MOMENTS

Some **key events** in the history of the New York Stock Exchange.

1790—The U.S. government issues $80 million in bonds to help refinance the debts accumulated during the Revolutionary War.

1792—The Buttonwood Agreement is signed, marking the beginning of what has become known as the New York Stock Exchange.

STOCK MOMENTS

Some **key events** in the history of the New York Stock Exchange.

1817—The New York Stock & Exchange is officially established, with its headquarters at 40 Wall Street.

1868—Membership in the NYSE is considered "property" that can be bought and sold at a price. The idea of buying and selling "seats" on the Exchange takes hold.

How Do Corporations Generate Cash?

Companies that issue stock to the public are considered "publicly held" or "publicly traded" corporations. Some companies choose not to sell their stock publicly and are considered "privately held" corporations. By selling shares of ownership to the public, the corporation generates cash to finance its operations and build business. Ownership of the company is widely distributed among shareholders. The corporation's management team is directly accountable to those shareholders, who are in effect the owners of the company. Companies that need additional cash can, to a point, issue more shares of stock to sell. If enough investors are interested in buying that stock, the company can continue to generate cash through this method. Corporations can raise cash in other ways, not the least of which is selling their products or services. A company's stock price is generally tied to its future profitability and cash flow more than any other single aspect of its business. The more product the company sells profitably, the more attractive that company's stock will be to investors. And this is where the rubber meets the road! If Wacky Widgees sells a million of those widgees at a dollar apiece, but it costs them two dollars to produce one, the company is not going to last very long unless it changes its cost structure in a radical way or raises the price of its products. But the company has a fine line to walk here; if it raises widgee prices too much, people will stop buying them, and the company will continue to suffer losses.

Consider Cash Flow

A company's cash flow is a critical factor to examine when you're looking for investment opportunities. Cash flow is like the flow of the ocean's tides. Sometimes the tide flows in, and sometimes the tide flows out. Any company is going to experience this

kind of ebb and flow in its cash situation, but if the tide flows out more than it flows in, eventually that ocean is going to dry up and the company will, like a beached whale, go belly up. If cash flow is balanced, the company can continue to survive, but it may be living on the edge until it can make more money. The ultimate goal of any corporation is to maximize positive cash flow so that more money is coming in than going out. If a company can successfully achieve this blissful state, it will have enough cash resources to continue operating, and perhaps even to expand and grow.

Why is cash so important to a company? Consider your personal finances, and then extrapolate to a much larger scale. Each person experiences cash flow, just as a corporation does. You get your paycheck every week or two, and then you have to take care of your bills, your rent or mortgage, your food, and any other items you need to purchase. If you've still got money left after you pay your bills, you have an overall positive cash flow, so you may be able to "expand your operations" by saving enough to buy a bigger house or a better car. On the other hand, if you have to borrow money just to stay afloat, you've got a negative cash flow situation. You don't have enough money to expand your operations, and you keep getting deeper into debt. If this pattern repeats itself for too long, it could end in bankruptcy.

Earning Profits through Capital Gains

One of the primary ways investors profit from the stock market is by earning money called "capital gains." Investors will continue to purchase shares of stock in a growing, profitable company, because the value of the company itself is increasing and therefore the value of owning shares in the company will increase. If you make money by selling a stock that has increased in value since you bought it, the money you earned is known as a capital gain.

A company's profitability is tied to its cash flow. Therefore, a company with a positive cash flow will be profitable, while a company with negative cash flow will not, regardless of the billions of dollars in sales that company may generate. So if widgees sell for a dollar but cost two dollars to make, your widgee company is not going to be profitable, and its stock will drop in value.

Investors are interested in finding companies that are profitable and growing because the value of their investment in that company is likely to increase as the value of the

corporation's business increases. Generally speaking, the stock of profitable companies will increase in value over time, because profitability means not only stability but also growth and increasing value.

Earning Profits through Dividends

Another way investors make money in the stock market is by receiving dividends. A dividend is a payment issued by a company to distribute to shareholders. When a company has become very profitable and stable and expects to remain so for the foreseeable future, its leaders may decide to pass along some of the profits to the stockholders who have helped finance the company all along. Most smaller companies don't pay dividends, because they need all the capital they can get to finance their growth. These companies usually reinvest their profits (if they have any) back into the business so they can keep growing and doing more business.

Larger, more established companies typically don't grow as much or as quickly as smaller companies, because they are farther along the growth cycle of the business. Just like babies who grow up to be children who grow up to be adults, companies experience growth phases that ultimately lead to maturity, if the company manages to survive in the long term. These mature companies often have steady and consistent revenues and cash flow and are therefore able to reward their investors on a more consistent and reliable basis by paying out dividends. The type of stock you find yourself investing in, a dividend stock or a growth stock, will depend on your investment objectives, your personal style, and your willingness to take on risk. But ultimately, you'll decide to invest one way or the other based on your expectations of where you'll make the most money in the safest (or quickest) possible way.

Because money is what the stock market is really all about. Money is the motivating factor that drives markets and investments and businesses around the world. Money is the basis of the national and the world economy. Money is what helps us get all the stuff we need and want as we journey through this material world. And money is certainly what makes the stock market go 'round or, more appropriately, up and down.

The stock market is, like any other market, a place where people can exchange things of value. In this case, people exchange shares of corporate ownership for money. As an individual investor in a very large marketplace, your first goal should be simple—to keep your head above water. After that, you're out to make a profit on your investment from dividends and capital gains.

A Brief History of the Stock Market

By this point, you're getting a clue about what this stock market thing is all about. The stock market is not actually one single market but many. The "stock market" that most people refer to consists primarily of four major markets or exchanges. Exchanges are actual places where people trade stocks, other securities, or commodities (like pork bellies and bushels of corn), just like people buy and sell things at any other market.

The two principal stock exchanges in the United States are the New York Stock Exchange (NYSE) and the American Stock Exchange (AMEX). Other large cities like Chicago, Boston, Philadelphia, Los Angeles, San Francisco, and Denver also have exchanges where people trade securities. The two other major stock markets are the Nasdaq National Market System and the small-cap market (typically referred to as over-the-counter markets), which generally handle stocks of less established companies with growth potential. These markets are not held in any particular location but are carried out either electronically via computer or directly between brokers or dealers. The newest additions to the stock market are alternative trading systems and Electronic Communications Networks (ECNs). These allow traders to link directly with other buyers and sellers to bid and offer shares in real-time via computer. International exchanges, such as the Tokyo and the London exchange, exist too, but this book will focus on the exchanges in the United States.

America's first stock exchange was organized in Philadelphia in 1790. At the time, Philadelphia was the country's capital. This first exchange flourished because of the great amount of government and business activity taking place in the capital city, and for a number of years Philadelphia was the primary exchange in the United States.

A couple of years after the Philadelphia exchange was founded, another exchange began to plant its roots in New York. At that time, Wall Street was little more than a dirt road that ran from Trinity Church down toward the dockyards of the East River. (Wall Street was so named because the road was flanked by a high wooden wall, erected in 1653 to protect the Dutch settlers from the attacks of both Indians and the British.) At the dockyards, people began trading bills of lading for the ships entering

STOCK MOMENTS

Some **key events** in the history of the New York Stock Exchange.

1886—On December 15, trading volume exceeds one million shares on the NYSE for the first time.

1913—The Federal Reserve System is established.

1929—The Great Depression begins as the stock market crashes, and stock values drop significantly.

and leaving the port as well as buying these bills of lading from each other with pieces of silver. The currency used for trading in those days was fragments cut from bars of silver or gold doubloons. The metal pieces were cut into eighths; thus the term, "pieces of eight." To this day, stocks continue to be traded in eighths as well as sixteenths and thirtyseconds, though some markets will soon move to decimals. As commerce in New York became more active, the securities market there began to grow.

In 1792, 24 brokers gathered under a buttonwood tree on Wall Street (so the legend goes) and drew up an agreement with one another to trade securities among themselves. They decided to charge a uniform commission rate to their customers for buying and selling those securities. The document these gentlemen signed is known as the "Buttonwood Agreement." This event marks the beginning of the New York Stock Exchange, although that name wasn't used until later. The Buttonwood Agreement was the first attempt to organize the often chaotic trading atmosphere of Wall Street.

As Wall Street grew and more buildings were built along the wall, the brokers and traders involved with buying and selling securities started moving into offices and conducting business indoors. By 1817, the members of the Buttonwood group had adopted the name "New York Stock & Exchange Board" (NYS&EB), and Wall Street had become the center of America's securities markets. In 1863, the name was shortened to the New York Stock Exchange, and the NYSE moved into the building that is still the current headquarters.

Meanwhile, outside on Wall Street another group of brokers was mobilizing. While the New York Stock & Exchange Board developed stringent rules about memberships and for listing stocks for trading, the Industrial Revolution was raging like an inferno, firing up the American economy and creating new companies and new industries never before imagined. Most of these companies needed funding to get their operations up and running, so they began to offer stock. But because the more conservative NYS&EB considered many of these companies too speculative, they were traded outdoors by brokers who weren't members. The market developed by this ragtag group became known as "The Curb" or "The New York Curb Exchange," because its trading activities took place outside, at the curb of the street. This market continued to exist outdoors until 1921, when the Curb Exchange moved indoors to its present location. In 1952, the name of this exchange was changed to the American Stock Exchange (AMEX).

The Purpose of the OTC Market

As the NYSE and AMEX grew, they became more institutionalized, with all the rules and accoutrements that accompany such institutionalization. This meant that listing a stock on either of these exchanges became more difficult for newer, less established companies that were just getting started. However, these companies, more than any other, needed the funding that offering stock to the public could provide. This need was handled by the OTC, or over-the-counter market, which really existed alongside the more established exchanges all along. This market operates in a manner very similar to that in which the major exchanges operated when they were first getting started: brokers trade directly with each other. These days, of course, no one stands outdoors on Wall Street to trade stocks, but brokers conduct their OTC transactions using telephones or computers. The OTC market handles stocks for very small companies, and their prices are listed daily on "pink sheets," which display pricing information for these stocks. This over-the-counter market is governed by a self-regulatory organization known as the National Association of Securities Dealers, or NASD.

Some of the companies whose stocks start out as low-priced and somewhat uncertain eventually grow and become more established corporations. When this happens, the company can attempt to have its stock listed on one of the major exchanges like the AMEX or NYSE. However, many companies prefer to keep their stocks listed on the OTC market. When an OTC stock becomes successful enough to fulfill certain criteria set by the NASD, it can then be admitted to the Nasdaq (National Association of Securities Dealers Automated Quotation) computerized system, which was developed in 1971 to provide real-time pricing information to the broker/dealers who trade these stocks. Currently, close to 5,000 stocks are tracked on the Nasdaq system, including such industry giants as Microsoft and Apple Computer. Nasdaq is a very efficient system that allows broker/dealers to get information about stocks quickly.

What's a Mutual Fund?

A mutual fund is a mechanism investors use to pool their money to buy stocks or other investments such as bonds. Pooling resources allows investors to purchase a larger number of shares, and it also enables them to invest in a greater variety of stocks than they could by themselves. This pool of resources is then managed for the investors by a professional money manager (or managers) who keeps a constant eye on the performance of the stocks in the fund, thereby (hopefully) reducing the risk involved and providing a greater overall return.

Another advantage of investing in mutual funds is diversification. While an individual investor may only have enough money to purchase shares of a few companies, the typical fund has enough resources to invest in dozens or even hundreds of companies. Diversification into a number of investments effectively lessens the risk involved in investing in a smaller number of stocks.

Imagine an investor who owns only two or three stocks. If one or two of those stocks go bad, that investor's entire portfolio has lost a great deal of value. If a few stocks go sour in a fund, the value of the fund doesn't suffer as much, assuming that the other investments in the fund do well. Of course, the converse turns out to be true as well; the fund won't benefit as much as the individual investor would from a great stock that appreciates significantly.

You have to assess your willingness to absorb risk when deciding on the type of investment to commit your dollars to. You also have to consider whether you think you'll be able to pick stocks that will appreciate over time or whether you'd rather leave that job to someone else. If your time is at a premium and you can't afford to do the homework required to be a successful stock investor, then you might want to consider a mutual fund.

They're All Connected

The major American trading venues (NYSE, AMEX, Nasdaq, and the OTC market) are also connected to the regional exchanges (such as the Chicago Stock Exchange) as well as to the international exchanges (like Tokyo or London) by computerized systems and telephones that allow traders to buy and sell almost any stock. So, while this thumbnail history focuses only on the stock market in the United States, remember that the stock market is actually quite international in scope.

The financial markets in one part of the world are affected by the markets in other parts of the world, so much so that a trend in one market is usually reflected in the others as well. You'll often hear commentators make remarks such as, "The London exchange fell today in sympathy with the happenings last night in New York." No exchange exists in a vacuum; the stock market is a broadly based yet tightly integrated international financial system. This marketplace not only provides companies with financing and investors with potential profits but also acts as a gauge for the health of all the economies of the world.

Swimming with the Sharks

From what you've seen so far, the stock market probably sounds like a consummately sane, rational marketplace that is run on sound business and ethical principles for the sake of keeping the wheels of commerce rolling smoothly along. Well, most of the time it works as it should, and the market is generally very efficient. But as with any enterprise involving large sums of money, unscrupulous individuals lurk about who will do anything to make a quick buck—even if their methods aren't quite ethical. And often they're on the lookout for someone like you: a person who may be clueless about the market but who's trying to get started. Dishonest but shrewd individuals can easily take advantage of those who are less knowledgeable by making unreasonable promises or by selling them something that they don't really want. One way to avoid being hoodwinked in the market is to learn as much as possible about how it all works and to find out who you're going to be dealing with along the way.

Most of the people you'll work with as you begin your excursions into the marketplace are ethical and reasonable people who, like you, are trying to make an honest profit by making the right investment choices at the right time. But you should learn up front

about the people that make this marketplace tick, so you'll be able to discern whether you're in the company of the genuine article or some kind of shyster. Of course, most shysters aren't wearing buttons that say, "Kick me, I'm a shyster," so you'll have to use common sense and your own intelligence (and the knowledge you're getting from this book!) to determine if you can trust someone. A key point to remember is that if you aren't comfortable dealing with a particular broker or company or salesperson, then you shouldn't do business with them. It's your money after all, and you should feel confident that you're working with someone who is on your side.

You Can Tell the Players with a Scorecard

So who are the players that make up the stock market? Here's a short list of the people you'll encounter as you play the market:

- *Full-service brokers.* These brokers are typically employed by full-service brokerage firms like Merrill Lynch or Paine Webber. A full-service broker may also be an independent financial advisor who has a seat on the exchange and is therefore able to execute orders directly for himself or his clients. Full-service brokers offer a great deal of useful information, advice, and a wide range of services, but all this comes at a price. The costs of using a full-service broker are usually higher than those involved with using discount or deep-discount brokers, but the service and advice they offer may make the expense worthwhile.

- *Discount brokers.* Discount brokers offer the investor the ability to buy and sell stocks at a lower price than full-service brokers charge. Of course, as with any cheaper product or service, you get what you pay for. You'll get a lot of information from a discount broker, but not a lot of service or advice. Therefore, you'll have to do more of your own research and stock evaluation. Examples of discount brokerage firms are OLDE Discount Brokerage and Charles Schwab.

- *Deep-discount brokers.* These brokers are the least expensive, but they will not hold your hand. Most of these firms offer only the most basic level of service, such as quarterly statements and an 800 number to call to place orders. Some of these firms operate only by computer, so that you can only place your orders by contacting the firm through the Internet or another computer network. If you are willing to make your own choices and your own mistakes without having someone to advise you, a deep-discount broker may be your best bet.

- *Broker/dealers.* This is a special class of brokerage firm that not only places buy and sell orders for customers but also sells stock that it keeps available in its own account or "inventory." These firms also deal heavily in new issues of stock. They purchase large quantities of stocks that they think will rise in value, then sell shares in those stocks to investors. If they can sell for more than they paid, they make a profit.

- *Specialists.* These individuals, functioning on an exchange such as NYSE or AMEX, are charged with the responsibility of maintaining a fair and orderly market in particular stocks by acting as both broker and dealer for those stocks, depending on the situation. Specialists are, in a sense, brokers to brokers. Each specialist is responsible for a small group of stocks and ensures that a buyer can always find a seller and a seller can always find a buyer for a stock. In the capacity of broker, for example, the specialist will take orders from other brokers that cannot be filled immediately because the price of the order is not at the current market price. The specialist will record the order and attempt to fill it later when pricing conditions come in line with the order. When the order is filled, the specialist will charge a commission for the service. As a dealer, the specialist will buy stock to keep the market moving and to prevent rapid price drops if there are many sell orders for a particular stock without corresponding buyers. Conversely, specialists will sell stock from their own account to fulfill buy orders if there aren't that many sellers.

- *Market makers.* This term refers to individuals when they are acting as dealers in particular stocks. A dealer, as you'll recall, sells stock from an inventory. Market makers buy or sell stocks to keep liquidity in the market for the stocks that they maintain. Market makers hope to profit by selling stock at a price greater than they paid for it.

- *Traders.* Traders are usually involved with buying and selling stock for their own accounts and their own profit. Also, some traders buy and sell stocks for large institutions such as mutual funds or brokerage firms.

- *Investment bankers.* Investment bankers, or underwriters, buy stock directly from corporations that are "going public." Then they attempt to re-sell that stock to investors, whether large institutions or individuals. They profit by selling the stock at a price higher than they paid for it as well as by charging underwriting fees to the corporation that is offering the stock.

Churning

As you can see, these various roles are all necessary to keep the markets moving and humming along with the activities of commerce. At the same time, you can see the potential for abuse that exists here. The stock market is a huge, bubbling money machine, and all those dollar signs tend to cast a hypnotic spell over the people that deal with them day to day. Everyone but the most austere and content individuals wants to make more money, and sometimes people are tempted to try to bend the rules to their advantage.

How does this happen? Consider brokers, for example. They make their take-home pay by generating sales for stocks. They're usually paid on a commission basis (or salary plus commission), and the commissions come from customer transactions, whether those transactions are buys or sells. If you call your full-service broker and ask to buy 100 shares of Microsoft, you're probably going to be charged anywhere from $20 to $100 for that transaction. Tomorrow, if you realize you've made a mistake and decide to sell those shares, you'll have to pay a commission for that transaction, too. So your broker has made, in two days, about $150 just by taking your orders. Whether or not you profit, the broker makes a commission.

When brokers advise clients to buy and sell in quick succession, with no apparent rhyme or reason, they may be guilty of "churning" accounts. Churning is the process whereby a broker generates a large number of transactions, profiting greatly from all the activity. If your broker seems to be getting you into and out of stocks very rapidly and frequently, you may want to ask what the purpose of all this activity is supposed to be. Of course, no broker will ever admit to churning an account, so you have to

keep your eyes open. Most brokers avoid this type of activity, because they would rather have valuable, potentially long-term customers instead of a source of quick commissions.

Price Manipulation

You should also watch out for the possibility of stock price manipulation. This occurs more frequently in stocks of very small, unestablished companies or companies that are financially on the rocks. A stock may have a very low price for a very good reason. The reason may simply be that the stock is practically worthless. On the other hand, it has been known for a market maker, dealer, or company insider (or anyone else with the resources to do so) to manipulate the price of such stocks by buying and/or selling inappropriately in order to make a profit at other people's expense.

For example, if XYZ stock has been trading at around 10 cents for the past few months, then suddenly you see the price shoot skyward (to, say, 15 or 20 cents) on a large volume of shares, don't jump into the stock without some careful investigation, regardless of who may be telling you that "you'll make a killing" on it and that "it's a sure thing." First, do some homework. Find out if the company's financial status has changed. If XYZ suddenly managed to pay off its incredibly huge debt and got a reputable bank to provide a solid and reasonable credit line to finance its business, you may be on to a company that is undergoing a genuine turnaround for the better.

Along the same lines, keep your eyes open for any good news that may affect the stock. If XYZ has just signed up a huge new customer for a long-term contract, that news may drive the price up. But if no news indicates that anything has changed for the better in the company's fortunes, and all you're hearing is your broker (who may be a market maker in XYZ, mind you) telling you that "this baby's going to the moon," well, let's just say you've been forewarned. If you are lucky enough to buy low and sell when

STOCK MOMENTS

Some **key events** in the history of the New York Stock Exchange.

1934—The Securities and Exchange Commission (SEC) is established to act as a watchdog agency over the markets.

1954—The Dow Jones Industrial Average finally passes the 1929 pre-crash high.

1970—The Securities Investor Protection Corporation (SIPC) is created to insure customers against losses from insolvency.

Interest and the Market

What is the relationship between the stock market and interest rates, and why should investors be aware of trends in these rates?

Most people who save money by putting it into a bank savings account, money market fund, certificate of deposit, or other such instrument think rising interest rates are wonderful. Imagine you have thousands of dollars in a savings account at 3 percent interest. If rates rise, you may find yourself suddenly earning 5 percent or more. That sounds great, right? Rising interest rates, while good for investments such as bank savings accounts, are terrible for the stock market.

Remember that interest rates affect more than just your bank account. Your credit card interest rate will usually rise as well, because many credit cards are tied to the prime rate, a general indicator of the direction of interest rates. Mortgage rates will also rise, making it more difficult for people to purchase or refinance their homes. Both of these situations are bad for business; if your credit card rate becomes outrageous, you're less likely to use it for purchases, and if no one is buying homes because of ridiculous mortgage rates, the construction industry suffers.

Also, high interest rates mean higher borrowing costs for businesses. If companies can't borrow money at reasonable rates when they need to, their businesses may suffer. Interest rates, however, are a classic example of the saying, "One man's trash is another man's treasure." People who are more conservative and invest in passbook savings accounts or other interest dependent investments will be pleased with higher rates.

the price has been driven up, you deserve a hearty congratulations and should thank your lucky stars that you escaped unscathed.

Usually, however, the scenario is not so pretty. The manipulator pushes the price up rapidly for a period of time, and you watch and watch as it climbs and climbs. Then, suddenly, your greed becomes unbearable, and you decide you've got to "get in on the action." Of course, that's likely the moment that thousands of other inexperienced investors will decide the same thing—and the same precise moment that the market manipulator will decide to dump all his holdings into an eager, gullible market. Soon after you've bought the stock, the great run-up will slow to a crawl or reverse itself altogether. Little by little, the stock price will trickle back down, and you'll either hang on for dear life and lose a great deal of money by getting stuck with worthless shares, or you'll sell in a panic when the stock gets back to 10 cents and lose a great deal of money from the sale.

The moral of the story? Learn as much as you can about a company before you invest, and make sure it is for real. Plenty of legitimate sources of information are out there for you, as you'll see later in this book. And remember, not all cheap stocks are bad either. A company may simply have fallen on bad times or may as yet be undiscovered. If you happen upon one of these gems, you'll be among the lucky few. At one time, even companies like Microsoft and McDonald's were cheap stocks. Imagine if you'd bought shares of those winners in their early days!

STOCK SEATS

What is an exchange "seat," and why would anyone want to sit there?

The New York Stock Exchange and the American Stock Exchange are private associations that offer memberships to individuals or organizations for a price. Aside from having intrinsic value, a seat on the exchange also grants the privilege of buying and selling stocks directly on the trading floor, without relying on an intermediary.

The price of an exchange seat varies over time. The price of a seat at the market's peak in 1987 was over a million dollars. In 1929 before the crash, the price of a seat was over half a million dollars. But in 1942, the price of a seat on the New York Stock Exchange was only $17,000.

Today, exchange seats are sold by auction and can sell for up to hundreds of thousands of dollars.

The vast financial ocean that is the stock market is full of all kinds of fish, some slippery, some smart and friendly, and some nasty buggers with big, sharp teeth. These fish are all very hungry, and the small fry are the easiest prey. If you venture cluelessly into the market, you can all but rest assured that you'll wind up on someone's dinner table, filleted, salted, and served with a wedge of lemon.

Knowledge is power, and the knowledge you need to make good in the stock market is available to you, if only you're willing to make the effort to seek it out and make use of it. To swim with the sharks, you have to understand how the sharks work and think, but you don't necessarily have to become a shark yourself. You do, however, have to be smart in your approach. Learn the rules, learn the ins and outs of the marketplace, and you'll not only survive, you'll prosper.

The Economy and the Stock Market

Because the stock market is the primary place for companies to get financing for their operations and one of the greatest places for investors to profit on the growth of those companies, the close relationship between the stock market and the economy as a whole is obvious. The strength or weakness of our economy is measured by various indicators that are standards of activity in economic sectors or the economy as a whole. Some of these indicators include:

- *Gross Domestic Product (GDP)*. A staggeringly large number that measures, in dollars, the total production of goods and services created by labor and property located in the United States during a specified period of time. When you hear the words "Gross Domestic Product" bandied about in the news, make sure you're paying close attention to the "Real GDP," because that number is inflation-adjusted and, therefore, more accurate.

- *Consumer Price Index (CPI)*. This index measures the changes in price of a group of goods and services purchased by all wage-earning consumers.

- *Unemployment rate*. A measurement of unemployment as a percent of the labor force during a specified period of time.

- *Retail sales*. A monthly measurement of total retail sales, in dollars, gathered from a voluntary survey of thousands of retail businesses across the country.

- *Business sales and inventories.* The sales portion of this index is comprised of the sum of sales in manufacturing, retail, and wholesale trade for a specified period. The inventories portion measures the amount of goods held in inventory by businesses that have yet to be sold.

- *Housing starts.* A measure of the number of homes that are beginning to be constructed during the measurement period.

- *Interest rates.* This is not a single measurement but rather a collection of measurements of various interest rates such as the Federal Funds Rate, the Discount Rate, the Prime Rate, and others.

- *Federal budget.* Usually discussed in terms of either a budget surplus or deficit, this indicator compares the spending of the federal government to the income it receives, primarily from income taxes.

- *Inflation/deflation.* Inflation is the rate at which the real cost of goods and services is rising in the economy; deflation is just the opposite.

Basically, these indicators measure business and consumer activity in the marketplace. The relationship between business and the consumer is this: If the business has something the consumer wants and the consumer has money to buy that thing, then a sale will be generated, and the business will profit from that sale. The leading economic indicators that you hear about all the time on the news are nothing more than measurements of this kind of activity on an enormous scale.

Consider the effort involved with trying to measure the buying and selling activities of hundreds of thousands of businesses, or the spending activities of millions and millions of people. That's exactly the kind of activity that is undertaken day after day by organizations such as the Bureau of Labor Statistics, the Bureau of Economic Analysis (BEA), and other groups that attempt to measure and quantify the national economy.

Interestingly, the stock market is not only directly affected by these indicators, but is also considered an economic indicator in its own right. Despite the apparent circularity of such measurement, the stock market is not only a primary barometer of economic health in a nation but also an area of the economy most sensitive to the goings-on in all other areas. The economic indicators are measurements of the buying and selling activities of companies and the spending and saving activities of individuals. The stock

market is affected by these activities because stock prices are driven by corporate earnings, which in turn are driven by consumer and industrial spending activities.

If customers aren't buying, then companies aren't selling, and stock prices generally aren't going up. Sometimes you'll see anomalies or irregularities in this relationship, but usually only in the short term. Over the long haul—meaning years—the stock market and the economy are tightly bound together; if the economy is strong, the stock market will be strong, and vice versa.

How Do the Primary Economic Indicators Relate to the Stock Market?

The GDP measures all economic activity in the country. The measurement is derived from considering the produce (meaning that which is produced, not fruits and vegetables) of all businesses, real estate, and the like. The stock market's primary concern is the profitability of corporations, so if the GDP shows strength and growth, generally the stock market will react positively and stock prices will rise. A strong GDP generally indicates strong corporate sales, which translate into corporate growth and profitability. The word "generally" is thrown in as an implicit caveat: If, for example, the GDP is strong but inflation or interest rates are rising rapidly as well, the stock market may react negatively. Why? Because high inflation will ultimately lead to a slowdown in sales when customers can no longer pay more and more for the things they want, causing corporate profits ultimately to slide, and then stock prices, and finally the GDP. If interest rates are rising, the market usually reacts negatively because high rates make it harder for companies to borrow money to finance growth or production. Rising interest rates also attract money away from stocks into CDs and bonds, which offer attractive rates of return at that point.

STOCK MOMENTS

Some **key events** in the history of the New York Stock Exchange.

1987—The stock market drops 508 points, or 22 percent, on October 19, the largest single-day percentage drop in the history of the stock market.

1992—The NYSE celebrates its 200th birthday.

The unemployment rate, retail sales, and the stock market all affect each other, too. The stock market's primary concern is generally corporate profitability as exhibited by positive cash flow over the long term. How would the stock market react to news of high unemployment? One of the economic effects of unemployment for those who are unemployed is a lack of disposable income. Disposable income is money that can be spent for any number of things, including discretionary, or unnecessary, purchases. If you lack disposable income, your primary concern is not going to be what fun and exciting new toys you can buy, but rather how the heck you are going to pay your bills. You may find that you need to keep your air conditioner off in the summer and your heat slightly lower in the winter, and you may try to stay off the phone as much as possible to avoid those costly long-distance charges.

If you cut back in all these ways, how will you affect companies that are trying to get their hands on your money? Their sad news is that they aren't going to get their hands on it. And if they don't get their hands on your money or your neighbor's money or anybody else's money, their retail sales go down the tubes. And if that happens, where is their profitability and cash flow? None of this looks so good for the shareholders. Not only will stock prices drop because of lack of corporate profitability but they'll drop as well because all of those unemployed folks will start cashing out of their investments in stocks and mutual funds so they can get together some money to pay their bills. And as corporate profits and sales decrease, corporations are more likely to fire or lay off employees, which makes unemployment go even higher, and the downward spiral keeps going downward.

But if unemployment were low and most people had jobs that paid well, people would have a great deal of disposable income, and they would just be itching to buy new toys. Spending would increase, which would drive up retail sales, which would drive up corporate profits, cash flow, and stock prices. People with disposable income not only spend money, they also invest it. That drives up stock prices even more. Profitable companies tend to be growing companies, and growing companies need to hire more people to keep their assembly lines humming along, and that will keep unemployment low.

Economic Cycle

There are five phases in the economic, or business, cycle: peak, recession, trough, recovery, expansion. The whole cycle is measured from peak to peak or from trough to trough, just as the phases of electromagnetic waves are measured.

Peak

The peak is the point at which the economy is the strongest. Business is booming, consumers are spending, the economy is quite strong, and everyone seems to think that things couldn't possibly go downhill. Often, when everyone starts to feel comfortable, the next phase begins. This phase is the beginning of the economic downturn, called recession. Why would a recession start if everything is looking so rosy? The cycle could begin to weaken for any number of reasons. For example, inflation might rise during the peak of the cycle. Why? If customers are buying everything in sight because they have a surplus of disposable income, eventually companies will say to themselves, "Selves, take a look around. Our customers are buying everything we produce and then some. Why don't we raise our prices to take advantage of our good fortune; we'll make more profit, and our shareholders will love us!" This strategy only works for a limited time; because eventually customers get fed up with paying even more for the merchandise they purchase. If people stop buying, companies stop selling, and then a recession begins as the economic cycle slows down.

Recession

A recession is a period in the economic cycle when business activity and spending are receding. The strength of the economy is on a downhill slide, and people are feeling a bit uneasy about their prospects. Consider the possible effects of a recession. A good example might be a business that sells discretionary products, things that are fun to have but not necessary for survival. If a recession begins, fewer people will buy these products and business will suffer. Because business suffers, the company may have to lay off employees just to break even and keep the doors open for another day. Laid-off people don't have a lot of spare cash lying around waiting to buy fun things, because they're having a hard time just paying the rent. Even fewer customers buy, and the company lays off even more employees, and if this downward spiral continues, the company may go out of business entirely. Now if this sort of thing happens to one company, that's bad luck for them. But if it happens on a national scale so that thousands of companies are going through it, then you have a recession.

Bottom

The bottom of the cycle is called the trough. This is where things look the bleakest for everyone. Just as at the peak when people were thinking nothing could ever go

wrong, at the trough nobody thinks anything will ever improve again.

Recovery

Just when all hope seems to be lost, the economy begins the next phase of the cycle, known as the recovery. A recovery is the period during which companies regain losses sustained during the recession and trough. This turnaround could be triggered by any number of factors. Let's imagine, for example, that our customers wake up one day, look around and say, "Gee, things have gotten really cheap because of the deflation that happened during the recession, and because my old car is getting really unsafe, I think I'll buy a new one." This assumes that the people who lost their jobs during the recession and trough have somehow managed to find other employment, and that they haven't been spending much during the hard times and so may have saved a few pennies for a down payment on that car. Eventually people find a way to stabilize their financial situation and start buying again, albeit slowly and cautiously. Companies start selling again and earning money, and eventually they find that they have to hire a few people to help manage the new influx of business. The recovery has begun.

TALK ABOUT AN ELECTRIC SLIDE

The largest single-day point loss so far recorded in the Dow Jones Industrial Average occurred on April 14, 2000, with a loss of 805 points, a total percentage loss of 7.3 percent of the entire valuation of the stocks in the average.

Expansion

The next phase is called expansion. During this period, the economic losses of the previous recession have all been recouped during the recovery phase, and now the economy is growing even beyond the level of the previous peak. This period is one of great economic activity, corporate growth, wage increases, and climbing stock prices. During a strong expansion, you'll probably notice the stock market indexes climbing fairly steadily because of earnings growth and profitability among corporations. The expansion is the phase that precedes the next peak, and there we return once again to the beginning of our cycle.

If you could buy stocks during the trough phase and then sell them during the peak, you'd do quite well in the stock market. But unless you're a psychic with an incredible

track record, you won't be able to predict the precise points at which the market begins to turn one way or another. This ability is called successful timing of the market, something that is rather rare in the world of investing.

Not an independent entity that is unaffected by the overall economy, the stock market is tied to the ups and downs of the business cycle and is also an indicator of the current phase of that cycle. As an investor, you need to keep up with what's going on in the world around you. All sorts of things affect the economy, from wars to crime to the price of oil and gasoline. Savvy investors take it upon themselves to find out more and put that knowledge to good use.

Capitalism at Its Best

The stock market is ultimately one of the purest expressions of capitalism in the modern world, a great result of the free market system that drives the American economy. According to the American Heritage Dictionary, capitalism is defined as "an economic system in which the means of production and distribution are privately or corporately owned and development is proportionate to the accumulation and reinvestment of profits gained in a free market." A key point of this definition is that development is directly related to profits. The free market system, capitalism, is at its core an economic system based upon the continuous and unbridled pursuit of capital, otherwise known as money. While this may sound negative, the fact is that this system is actually productive, very efficient, and produces a lot of wealth.

The free market system was the primary reason that countries like the United States, Japan, and most of Western Europe have developed such strong economies with high standards of living. And while the word "unbridled" is not strictly true (plenty of laws, regulations, and rules limit abuse), for the most part the market is left to its own devices, with buying and selling taking place among individuals and companies and institutions with a minimum of governmental or external control. If you look around the world today, you'll see countries that have for many years disdained the capitalist system as somehow "evil" suddenly embracing free market thinking, because despite all its faults, it is historically the most efficient economic system that has ever existed. In short, it works. And the stock market is one of the greatest fruits of that system.

THE *nuts* and bolts of *how it* WORKS

CHAPTER TWO

Now that you've gotten an overview of what the market is and how it fits into the **larger scheme** of things, you're probably itching to get down to some details. How does it work? How do things **fit together?**

Where's your place in all of this number crunching financial activity? Not to inflate your ego, but the fact of the matter is that if you're a shareholder of a company, you are an owner of that company. You and a few hundred thousand other people collectively own that company, with all the rights and responsibilities that go along with that ownership.

Equity

Equity is a term that means "ownership" or "having a stake" in something. For example, if you rent an apartment, you have no equity in it because you don't own any part

of that space. You rent the apartment, which means that you pay a certain amount of money for the right to stay there for a period of time. By contrast, if you own a condominium or a house, you have equity, or ownership, of that space. You can do whatever you want in there, and the only person you will affect is you. You can sell the condominium whenever you want, and if you do, you'll get something back of what you originally put in and may perhaps even make a profit.

Stocks are considered equity investments because you, as an investor, have a stake in the ownership of that company. But just because you own part of that company doesn't mean you can go into the boardroom and tell everyone how to run the place. Your percentage of ownership is probably quite small in comparison to the percentage a large mutual fund company owns or that of the founder of the company, who may have as much as 50 percent or more ownership.

You may be asking, "What? The founder only owns 50 percent of the company? How the heck did that happen?" That happened because the founder of the company, being a smart and savvy businessperson, realized that to grow the company beyond the initial startup phase, the business required a large infusion of capital to finance that growth. A number of financing alternatives exist, but in the real world, a business often finds it difficult to get bank credit or other types of loans when it's starting up. Most lenders are interested in maximizing the security of their loan investments. Banks would rather loan money out at 5 percent and have a fairly high level of confidence that they'll get their money back with that interest, than lend money at 10 percent with a higher possibility of not getting any of the money back. Banks tend to be rather conservative investors, so the hot new widget company's president may have trouble convincing the bank that the company is really going to make millions of dollars selling those awesome widgets. In lieu of bank credit, the company might be able to issue bonds, which are a method of borrowing money from investors. But again, bond investors tend to be more conservative than stock investors, so the start-up may have difficulty selling those bonds.

So what is an ambitious entrepreneur to do? The primary value of the start-up is the company itself, so why not exchange some of the ownership of the company for dollars that can be used to finance growth? While the owner trades some of the ownership of the company to investors, who may be strangers, thus losing the privilege of 100 percent ownership, the upside is the benefit of additional capital that can be reinvested in the company, thus fostering growth. While it seems unfortunate that the owner loses some control over the company, the entrepreneur's success will be greatly enhanced if the company can grow significantly, even if the owner has a smaller piece of the whole pie. A 50 percent piece of a million dollar pie is a lot nicer than a 100 percent piece of a hundred thousand dollar pie. Another benefit is that investors often bring certain expertise, resources, and experience to a start-up, all of which can be put to good use to expand a growing business.

How Do Companies Find Investors?

It all depends on the type of investors the company is looking for and the amount of money the company needs to finance its planned expansion. Imagine that your friend Joe decides to open a pizza business. Joe has managed to save a chunk of money over the years from his regular job, and now he wants to bite the bullet and say good-bye forever to the stodgy corporate life he's been living. Joe rents some space, buys or leases equipment, comes up with a killer pizza recipe that even you think is fantastic, hires a few people to help out, and then, a week after opening day, realizes that it just might take a while before the crowds start forming outside the door. He's getting some customers, but Joe has finally figured out that there's more to building this pizza business than simply having a great tasting pizza. For one thing, Joe needs to get the word out to the public that his terrific pizza joint is now open for business. While you and all your friends have eaten there a few times already (in a gesture of moral support, but also because you really like his pizza), the fact is that your circle of friends isn't going to be able to drum up enough interest by word of mouth, even though you already know that Joe's is the best darned pizza place this side of town.

Joe decides he needs to advertise in the city paper. The problem is, of course, that by now most of Joe's savings have disappeared into renting the store, getting equipment, and paying the salaries of his employees. And while Joe was initially confident that sales would rapidly grow to the point where he'd have plenty of income to keep the business running, he's quickly discovered that he needs more money not only for advertising, but just to keep the doors open for a few more days. So, being a good-natured, trusting soul, Joe trudges down to his local bank and asks his banker for a loan. The banker's first question is, "What are your annual sales?" Joe sheepishly replies, "I don't know. I've only been in business for a couple of weeks." This lack of a

track record does nothing to satisfy the banker's curiosity about how Joe plans to pay back the loan. Joe's enthusiastic, "We're going to be the biggest pizza chain in the state!" unfortunately falls on deaf ears. Joe sadly drags himself back to the pizza parlor and fears that his dream may soon crumble to dust at his feet.

Next morning, Joe gets a brilliant idea: he'll ask to borrow money from his friends! They love the place, and they'll be glad to help out. When he asks for loans, however, he gets just about the same response that he got from the banker. Perplexed by this lack of support, but still untiring in his determination, Joe offers to let his friends have a stake in the business if they give him some money. Joe's friends start to show more interest, because now he wants to make them partners. The dollar signs start flashing before their eyes. Yes, they take a risk that the business will fall apart and they'll lose their investment, but on the other hand, if the business does well, everybody wins. As creditors, if Joe's business had fallen apart, they'd have lost everything as well, but if Joe made millions, they'd only get their money back with interest. As investors, they'll get to share in the wealth, so their investments might end up making them rich. Five of Joe's friends decide to contribute $5,000 each, and Joe draws up an agreement that gives them each 5 percent of the ownership of the company. Joe's given up 25 percent of his ownership, but now he has $25,000 to use for advertising and to pay his bills.

Joe hasn't issued any stock officially because he hasn't yet incorporated his business, but he has sacrificed some ownership to get financing. His business has made the transition from a sole proprietorship where he was the only owner to a partnership where ownership is distributed between or among individuals.

Incorporating

This transition is not an unusual scenario for a brand-new business. But as the business grows, Joe decides he wants to incorporate, a process in which a business becomes registered with the state as a corporation. A corporation is a form of business considered to be an independent entity, like a person, that has legal rights and responsibilities apart from the individuals that own it. As a business grows, the potential liability from lawsuits tends to grow as well, because the business has more employees, more locations (for stores like Joe's), and more people using (or eating) its products. In a sole proprietorship or partnership, if the company is sued and loses the suit, the owners may lose their own personal property if the company is required to pay off that

judgment. In the meantime, while you've been here reading about corporations and stocks, Joe has increased his business to fill three stores, and now has 50 employees!

A corporation is a good legal structure for Joe's pizza stores, because if something terrible happens, the responsibility will lie with the company as an independent entity, not with him and his partners as individuals. By incorporating, Joe will be able to sell shares of stock to the general public, gaining an additional source of income to finance his planned statewide expansion. Not that he couldn't ask his friends or family for more assistance of course, but Joe has become very ambitious, and his plans call for a great deal more money than he'd be able to scrounge up just from his group of loyal friends.

EVER HEAR OF THE "KENNEDY PANIC"?

In 1963, the White House pressured a number of large steel companies, including U.S. Steel, into reversing a $6 per ton increase in the price of steel. Many investors considered the actions of the government to be antibusiness. This event was a key contributor to a six-month slide in the markets that caused the Dow's value to drop by 27 percent.

To incorporate, Joe has to decide in which state he wants to base his business, because some states offer better conditions for small businesses than others, even if that business has its headquarters somewhere else. Once that decision has been made, he'll need to contact the state government and get some forms and documents to complete and return to the state (with some money for fees). Joe handles all the details like a pro (or he hires a lawyer to help him), and the next thing you know Zza, Inc. is officially launched as a corporation in Joe's home state, with Joe as the president.

Venture Capitalists and Private Placements

As a corporation, Zza can offer stock to the public. One possibility is that the company will sell stock in a "private placement." For example, if some wealthy investors hear about Joe's grand expansion plans and think he'll pull it off successfully, they may strike a deal with Joe for a certain number of shares of the company's stock in exchange for a very large investment of cash. Groups of investors do this sort of thing on a regular basis, and companies called venture capital firms specialize in investing in new,

growing businesses with the sole purpose of ultimately making a great profit from the investment.

So Joe agrees to sell another 24 percent of his company to a venture capital firm for $500,000, leaving him with only 51 percent of the ownership, because the initial partners received a total of 25 percent of the stock when they signed the partnership agreements. Joe has decided that he wants to be the "majority shareholder" so he can maintain most of the control of the company, and that's why he kept at least 51 percent of the shares. In many cases, however, the venture capital firm will buy larger portions of ownership, and sometimes will even become the majority shareholder of the corporation. Every deal is different.

Going Public

In time, Zza grows and grows and all the investors are happy because of the great profits they're making. Soon Zza has 40 stores throughout Joe's home state, and Joe decides it's time to take his Zza nationwide. Joe consults his accountant and his lawyer, and they recommend an investment banker. The professionals all agree it's time for Zza to "go public." By offering shares to the broader market, Joe's little miracle will accumulate enough capital for the national expansion campaign he's waited years to begin. The investment banker's role will be to advise Joe on the number of shares to offer as well as to suggest a reasonable price that can be expected per share. In addition, the underwriter will ensure that all appropriate legalities are handled and ultimately will be responsible for selling the shares to public investors. The investment bank will offer 51 percent of Joe's shares to the public at an initial price of $10 per share. If all goes well, the stock offering sells through and Zza has enough money to start building stores in other states. In time, as the company continues its tremendous growth and investors trade the stock on the exchange, the value of shares of stock in Zza increases. By now, Joe's personal stake in Zza has dwindled to just 25 percent of the total number of outstanding shares, but the value of those shares has increased exponentially, and Joe is one happy pizza man.

The Initial Public Offering (IPO)

When you hear that a company is "going public," it means that the company is issuing shares of ownership for sale in the public marketplace. This process takes place during the initial public offering, or IPO. The IPO is a first-time offering of stock for sale to the general public. The IPO process involves a number of people in addition to the company owners and can be a rather complex undertaking.

To begin with, the company that wants to go public must contact an investment banking firm (or a group of investment banking firms working together as a syndicate) that is willing to underwrite the public offering. The investment banking firm's responsibilities are key to the success of the offering. Their first step, once they agree to underwrite the offering, depends on the track record of the company going public and the expectation of success for the stock offering. In the case of a risky business or one that is not well established, the underwriter may offer the stock on a "best efforts" basis. Best efforts means that the underwriters will do their best to sell the stock, but if they are unable to find enough buyers, they are not required to sell all the stock the company issued. The underwriter may also reserve the right to sell the offering on an all-or-none basis, which means that if they can't find buyers for all the stock to be issued, they may call off the entire offering. The underwriter's profit in this case is generated by a commission charged for selling the stock. If the underwriter agrees to a firm commitment to sell the entire offering, usually the first move is to buy all the shares that are going to be publicly offered from the selling company at an agreed-upon price. The underwriter then attempts to sell those shares to the public for a higher price, thus profiting from the transaction.

Once the type of arrangement between the investment banker and the company has been determined, the investment banker will file a registration statement or full disclosure statement with the Securities and Exchange Commission (SEC). This is required by law and must include in-depth details about the company. The registration includes information like a statement of business purpose, how management intends to grow the business, the number of shares of stock the company is selling, and what the company plans to do with the money earned from the IPO. Once the disclosure statement is accepted by the SEC, it becomes the official prospectus of the offering. The prospectus is then used by the investment banker as a sales tool and to provide information to interested investors.

During the registration process, the investment banker or syndicate will work with prospective investors to determine an appropriate selling price for the new shares. A good price is one that will make both the issuer and the investors happy. However, this

can be a difficult compromise, because the issuer and the underwriter want to get as much money as possible, but investors want to pay less for the stock they buy. Once the price is determined, the investment banking firm publishes a public notice of the offering, called a tombstone, so named because it's somber and to the point, without any advertising flash or pizzazz. When the effective date of the offering comes, the shares are sold to investors. Typically, however, orders are taken and shares are already spoken for in advance of this date. After the effective date, and when all the shares have been distributed, the stock trades publicly on an exchange or OTC market, where any investor can purchase shares.

Distributing Wealth and Responsibility

Distribution of wealth is one of the great effects of the stock market. Because many people can get involved, many people can also experience significant profits if their investments are fruitful. While the founder of a successful corporation like Zza can wind up a very rich person, growing corporations generate wealth and economic prosperity for many other people as well. All those investors who helped Joe get his business off the ground in the early stages were richly rewarded when Zza became a success, as were the venture capitalists and investors who got involved a little later in the game. And they deserve to have been rewarded. These people risked their money to help an unproven business idea get off the ground, and when it did, their risk paid off for them handsomely. Distribution of wealth creates greater prosperity for the nation as a whole, because more people possess the means to purchase additional goods and services, which in turn increases corporate profits. This cycle is what drives the economy.

The wealth generated by the growth of successful companies doesn't occur only through the actions and existence of the stock market. Growing companies create wealth and prosperity because of the wider influence they have on society as a whole. Imagine Joe's Pizza at its very beginnings. Joe hired two or three people to help out with deliveries and to make pizzas. These few people benefited from his efforts because they were able to get steady jobs that helped them pay their bills. As Zza grew to be a corporation of immense proportions, the jobs created by that company numbered in the thousands across the country. All were jobs that did not exist previously, and possibly might not have existed at all were it not for the success of Zza. While you might not consider pizza delivery jobs to be capable of creating wealth, you have to allow the

possibility that those people had no jobs before Zza hired them. This means that those jobs represent a level of prosperity that did not exist before.

A successful company often spurs the growth of other successful companies. The economic effects of a growing company extend far beyond the walls of the company itself, and the employees and owners are not the only people to benefit from that growth. Pizza is made of various components like flour, sausage, tomato sauce, and other ingredients. Joe's company buys these ingredients literally by the ton because of the size of his overall operation. Well, one of Joe's friends just happened to have started a sausage company around the time Zza was really taking off. The business from Joe's company in itself was enough to make his friend's sausage company one of the biggest in the Mid-

IS NEW YORK REALLY SO BIG?

Everyone knows that New York City is often fondly referred to as the "Big Apple." But did you know that the New York Stock Exchange is frequently called the "Big Board"? Is New York really so big? It's not the biggest city in the world, but the **NYSE** is certainly the biggest and busiest stock exchange.

west, but because of the reputation Joe's friend gained by being Zza's sole sausage supplier, he has signed contracts with a number of Joe's competitors as well. And then there's the flour company, and the tomato sauce company, and the oregano company. All of Joe's drivers need cars, so they all buy new Chevys or Saturns. Every one of Joe's stores has two pizza ovens, 100 tables with four chairs each, and hundreds of red-and-white checkered tablecloths.

The wealth created by a company generates jobs for workers, prosperity for communities, and wealth for investors and entrepreneurs, and it spurs the growth of the entire national economy. This all relates directly to the stock market, because the stock market is driven by the economy and the economy is driven by the stock market. It's a great round of economic interdependence that depends completely on the growth of successful businesses like Zza.

Establishing a Board of Directors

The board of directors is a group of individuals that is responsible for managing the affairs of the corporation, because there's more to corporate growth than the genera-

tion of wealth. In order for all this managing to happen, someone has to manage the business as it grows. The responsibility for managing a small company usually rests with the founder or owner of that company and perhaps any management team that the entrepreneur assembles. As a company grows ever larger, however, the responsibilities of management become greater. This increase in responsibility is directly proportional to the amount of expansion the company is undergoing. A very large, fast-growing company requires more management effort than a small, lethargic company. A corporation that has issued stock publicly has another advantage over a privately held corporation in that the responsibilities of management are distributed among the shareholders of the corporation. In addition to hiring experienced management, the public company has a board of directors, which is elected by the shareholders.

The power of the board of directors usually extends even beyond that of the founder or company president (a situation which some company presidents don't always regard as positive). However, this power resides in the board because the board represents the shareholders. The shareholders of a public company are the true owners of that company, regardless of what the person who founded the company might like to think. And the company's president and management team are ultimately accountable to those owners.

The board of directors typically consists of the shareholders who own the greatest number of shares (a group that often includes the founder or president) as well as a number of "outsiders" added to the mix for balance and perspective. The board is sometimes self-appointed, in the sense that the major shareholders also have the greatest number of votes and can influence the outcome of elections more than minority shareholders can. If the founder and his partners own a majority of shares (greater than 50 percent of the total number of shares), they can effectively control the company. As long as they agree on how elections should turn out, they'll always be able to elect themselves to board positions and therefore maintain their control. However, if the owner does not personally control a majority of shares, and the other members of the board decide that she is not doing such a hot job anymore, they might oust her from the presidency.

While ousting the owner may sound cruel or bizarre, sometimes it's necessary to keep the company going strong. Stories abound about company founders who were terrific

entrepreneurs, possessing the ability to build up a company from just a few pennies in their pocket, but turned out to be terrible managers as the company matured. The distribution of responsibility that comes with the distribution of ownership provides a mechanism whereby a company can outlive its founder if that founder proves to be unable to handle the job. While this may seem unpleasant to the founder, it can be good news for shareholders.

Ownership: What's in a Share?

Buying shares of stock makes you an owner of the company that issued the stock, and ownership gives you a stake in the equity, or total value, of the corporation. If you've bought stock before, you might be thinking that ownership really doesn't amount to a whole bunch of anything except maybe a few dividends and perhaps the appreciation of the value of the stock. In a sense, you're right—the ownership of individual investors is such a small percentage of the total equity of the company that for all practical purposes they have no control over the company's direction. Larger shareholders usually have much more decision-making power and often are elected to positions on the board because of their greater influence. Yet, despite the fact that sometimes small shareholders feel somewhat isolated from the inner workings of the company, they do have rights and responsibilities.

One of the rights you have as an investor is the right to vote for the board of directors as well as important company issues. Normally, owning one share of common stock gives you the power of one vote. If you control a larger number of shares, you'll have more influence on the outcome of elections. For example, if Zza, Inc. were to decide to expand their operations by adding a line of frozen pizzas for retail markets, they could call a shareholder vote on the issue because it's such a major change in the general direction of the business. Another reason companies call for a vote is if they want to issue additional shares of stock to the public to raise more money.

Shareholders also have the right to attend the annual meeting, which is where the voting is usually done. You don't actually have to attend the meeting to cast your vote, however. Most shareholders vote by proxy, which is basically an absentee ballot. If you aren't planning to be at the meeting, you fill out the proxy ballot and send it in before the elections take place.

Types of Stock

Corporations issue different classes of stock, and each has a different "weighting" of votes. If Joe wants to maintain control of Zza, even though he knows that after the public offering of shares he'll only have 25 percent of the total number of shares outstanding, he can arrange to set up different classes of common stock with different rights pertaining to each class. If he plays his cards right, he can keep the shares with the greatest voting rights, maintaining control of the company although he owns less than a majority of the total shares outstanding. If Joe holds shares that are assigned voting rights equivalent to three of the "lower class" shares, for example, he'll be able to keep the reins of power. Another way for entrepreneurs to keep control is to issue some shares that have no voting rights at all. This sort of differentiation between classes of common shares is relatively rare, but it may be in your best interest to read the public statements made by the companies in which you're investing to see just how things work in their particular case.

Receiving Dividends

Another right of shareholders is the right to receive dividends. Successful companies with consistent positive cash flow may decide to share their profits directly with shareholders in the form of a dividend, a method companies use to distribute profits among their shareholders. While it is the right of shareholders to receive these dividends if they are declared, it is by no means required that the company pay out dividends at all. The board of directors has complete control over the question of dividends in a corporation, and the officers of the company are under obligation to comply with the board's decision. If the board decides it's time the shareholders started sharing directly in the profits of the company, it may declare an annual dividend paid out quarterly. The declaration is the decision to pay dividends and the formal announcement of that intention is given to shareholders as a written notice.

Suppose Zza has become such a fixture in the American culinary landscape that it consistently earns large profits. However, the company is not growing as much as it was during its hottest expansion phase. In this period of the company's existence, it is not as crucial that the profits be reinvested to finance growth, so the board decides to declare an annual dividend of $1 per share. This means that every quarter, usually

Common versus Preferred

Many companies issue two different types of stock: common stock and preferred stock.

When you buy stock for your own investments, you'll usually purchase **common stock.** The term common doesn't carry any negative connotations but rather indicates that it is the "standard" stock that the company has offered. The other type of stock is called preferred, not because the company necessarily likes those shares better, but because the shares offer investors privileges and rights that are different from those offered by common stock.

Preferred stock tends to be safer than common stock for two primary reasons. First, a fixed dividend is paid to owners of preferred shares before any additional dividends can be paid to owners of common stock. Second, if a company goes out of business, the owners of preferred shares have prior claim to any assets that remain when the company is dissolved, after bond owners and other creditors have been paid. Owners of common stock are the last in line to pick up the pieces of a fallen corporation.

Owning preferred shares has disadvantages as well. Preferred shares carry no voting rights. Also, the price of preferred shares tends to rise more slowly than the price of common shares, so preferred shareholders may profit less than owners of common shares if the company grows.

around the time quarterly earnings are announced, shareholders get a check from Zza. If you own 100 shares, your dividend will be for $100 per year, payable at $25 per quarter.

Residual Rights

Residual rights apply to those unfortunate situations in which a company is dissolved. As an owner of the company, you have the right to receive any part of the proceeds that results from dismantling the corporation. However, this right applies to owners of common stock only after other interested parties' rights are satisfied. This means that if a company falls apart and has to close its doors forever, you, as an owner of common stock, are at the end of the line of people with their hands out waiting for a piece of what's left.

First, all salaries must be paid to employees. Then, any outstanding taxes must be taken care of. Next in line are the company's creditors, and then owners of preferred stock will get their bit of the carcass. And last, and in this case least, the owners of common stock will get the rest. Unfortunately, if the company is going out of business, it often doesn't have enough even to pay back all the taxes and salaries, let alone the shareholders. And this is the biggest risk you face as an owner. In most cases, if the company goes out of business, the stockholders will lose their entire investment, because so many other people pick up the pieces of the fallen company before the stockholders even get the chance to see what pieces are left.

The greatest benefit of stock ownership is the implicit right to share in the growth of a successful company by owning a stock that appreciates in value over time as the company grows. This right means that if you buy stock in Zza at $5 a share when its growth phase is still young, hold the stock through its national expansion phase, and finally sell it when it hits $75 a share, you have made a substantial profit on your investment because, as a company owner, you share in the profitability of that company. This seems obvious and quite simple, and you're probably wondering why more people aren't millionaires from investing in stocks. Although the concept is simple, the execution of your investment decisions determines whether or not you're a successful investor.

Stocks versus Bonds

Stocks are equity investments, meaning that one share of stock gives you ownership in the corporation that issued that stock. Bonds, on the other hand, are a form of debt assumed by the issuing party and are known as fixed income investments or debt securities. A bond is like an IOU from the issuer to the purchaser that indicates the issuer will repay the purchaser over time for the loan, with interest. Bonds, unlike stocks, are not only issued by corporations but are also issued by the federal government as well as state and municipal governments. Bonds allow people to invest their money as a loan to the issuer in return for a stable rate of interest.

Another difference between stocks and bonds is that because a bond is a form of loan, the owner of a corporate bond is among the first to receive any proceeds from the dissolution of a company if it should go out of business. In this sense, bonds are safer investments than stocks, particularly common stocks. On the other hand, bond investors don't share in the wealth generated by a fast-growing company. While the selling price or value of a bond may increase if the issuing company has become very successful, it won't appreciate nearly as much as the price of stock in the same situation.

The principle at work here is risk versus reward. Investments with higher risk have the potential for greater rewards. However, the factor of risk means that if a company goes out of business, a bondholder has a better chance of getting a piece of the investment back, whereas the owner of common stock will probably lose the entire investment.

Bonds issued by the federal government are considered to be among the safest of all investments because they are backed by the "full faith and credit of the U.S. government." They are issued in three forms: Treasury bonds, Treasury bills, and Treasury notes. Other bonds include municipal bonds, which are issued by cities. The greatest benefit of "munis," other than their relative safety, is the fact that they are exempt from federal taxes and may be exempt from state taxes if the purchaser lives in the state in which the issuing municipality is located.

Stock Splits: Why and Wherefore?

A split isn't something physical that happens to stock certificates. Rather, it is something that companies may decide to do if their stock has been very successful. In effect, a split increases the number of shares of stock outstanding, but it does nothing to change the total market value (calculated by multiplying the total shares outstanding by the price per share) of the company. For example, suppose Wacky Widgees has a total of 10 million shares of stock outstanding, at a price of $50 per share. If Wacky's board of directors decided to do a two-for-one split and the shareholders approved it, they'd have 20 million shares of stock outstanding at a price of $25 per share. The company's market value remains the same ($500 million), but current shareholders now have twice as many shares, and new investors can buy shares at a lower price. Stocks can be split in any number of ways; two-for-one, three-for-two, three-for-one, and so on. The decision rests with the company.

The reason a company would choose to split its shares is primarily to stimulate trading and to enable smaller investors to buy shares. Because most investors buy shares in round lots (a block of 100 shares), because commissions are sometimes higher for odd lot transactions (blocks of anywhere from 1 to 99 shares), it would be difficult for smaller investors to buy shares of a company whose stock is priced at $150. If that company splits its shares four-to-one, however, the price would drop to $37.50 per share, making it easier for smaller investors to buy that company's stock. The market value of the company hasn't changed, but the total number of outstanding shares has increased by a factor of four.

STOCK TECH

These major **technological advances** have affected the stock markets.

1867—First ticker in use

1883—First electric lights in use

1903—First pneumatic tubes in use

Often a stock's price will rise somewhat after a split, perhaps because investors become more interested in the stock and that interest causes a wave of buying. A stock split is generally perceived as a positive indicator for a stock as well, because stocks that are doing poorly usually are priced low to begin with.

A reverse split has the opposite effect of a normal split. Instead of increasing the number of shares outstanding and decreasing the share price, a reverse split decreases the number of shares outstanding while at the same time increasing the price of the stock. While this type of split is not looked upon very favorably by many investors, particularly investors who already own shares of that stock (because the number of shares they own decreases), sometimes a company needs to do a reverse split. Consider a company that has 200 million shares of stock outstanding and has fallen on hard times over the past year or so. The stock price may have dropped to $.50 per share, because investors have sold large quantities of stock and demand for the stock has become practically nil. While smaller investors often seek less expensive shares, because they are more affordable, shares that are priced this low are considered highly risky. In addition, institutional investors such as pension funds, insurance companies, and mutual funds will avoid penny stocks such as this because of their high risk.

Now suppose that new management has taken control of the company and has made changes that are likely to make the company successful again. In order to stimulate investor interest, the board of directors may approve a reverse split. If this company approves a one-to-ten reverse split, the total number of shares outstanding will decrease to 20 million, and the share price will increase to $5 per share. Not only is the price more attractive at this point, but fewer shares means that it will take a smaller number of shares traded to make significant changes to the price and the price can rise more quickly on positive news. Be careful about buying stock after a reverse split, though. Because reverse splits are considered negative events, at least initially, the stock price often drops immediately after a reverse split.

Your Uncle Wants a Piece of the Pie

What if you did make $70 a share on your investment in Zza? Successful investors often find everyone around them clamoring for just a little taste of that big slice of pie these investors have managed to cut for themselves. And the guy with the biggest hand out is your Uncle Sam from Washington—the federal government wants to make sure it gets a sizable chunk of the pie, even before you get to play with your profits yourself.

Stock investors need to consider a number of tax issues when they buy and sell stock. Tax liability is an issue of concern to all investors, so you should learn at least the basics of what is required of you. However, because tax laws change with the political

How Activity in the Bond Market Affects the Stock Market and Vice Versa

While stocks and bonds are fundamentally different types of investments, they don't exist in a vacuum. Activity in the bond market affects the stock market and vice versa. Historically, an inverse relationship exists between bond prices and stock prices. Bonds are debt securities, so as interest rates rise, the selling price of new bonds will increase because the interest they pay out will be higher. But when interest rates rise, stock prices tend to decline because interest rates are bad news for corporate earnings.

When corporations have to pay higher interest rates for loans, they may opt not to borrow money to grow their operations but rather wait for better times. If interest rates rise and a company issues bonds, it will have to sell the bonds at a discount to match the market interest rate. Otherwise, investors will elect to purchase another company's bonds that pay the higher market interest rates.

But low rates are good news for stock investors because as borrowing costs decrease for companies, they can afford to borrow money for growth. And growth often leads to higher stock prices.

climate and are often quite complex, you'd be well advised to seek the assistance of a qualified accountant or tax attorney when you are preparing your taxes. In particular, you should be aware of events in your investing career that will require you to pay taxes, or not pay taxes, as the case may be.

Any income you earn from stock investing is taxable. For example, the quarterly dividends you receive from a dividend-paying stock are taxable, generally at the rate at which you pay your normal income tax. Some dividends are considered "optional" dividends, which means that you can take your dividend payout in shares of stock instead of in cash. These dividends are immediately taxable, whether you take your payment in cash or in shares. The other form of dividends is nonoptional dividends, which are usually paid out as additional shares of stock. You are not immediately responsible for paying taxes on these as you are with optional dividends, but you may be liable for taxes when you sell the shares.

The tax rate on dividends is currently the same as the rate on regular income. In all cases, you are responsible for reporting and paying your taxes on dividends. If you neglect your responsibility, chances are Uncle Sam will know about it. Corporate dividends are a matter of public record, and your ownership of stock is registered with your brokerage firm. The brokerage firm gives you and the government an annual report on the amount of dividends you have received on an IRS 1099 form. If you're avoiding a tax liability, the IRS will have no trouble finding out about it.

Capital Gains Taxes

When you sell your stock for a profit, the money you earn from this transaction is known as capital gains. There are two types of capital gains: short-term and long-term. A short-term capital gain is a gain from selling an investment you have owned for one year or less. (The period of time used to define "short term" has fluctuated through the years—it's been as short as 6 months and as long as 18 months.)

Short-term capital gains are currently taxed at the standard income tax rate to a maximum of 39.6 percent, as opposed to 20 percent for long-term gains. Politicians discuss capital gains taxes frequently, and the rates may change again in the future. A lower capital gains tax encourages additional investment, which is good for the economy.

But legislators must consider a number of issues when they determine the tax laws, and some of these considerations include providing enough revenue to keep the wheels of government rolling.

What If I Lose Money in the Stock Market?

People will always find you more interesting if you've made money in the market than if you've lost it, and the government is certainly no exception. However, current tax law offers one cushion that can help alleviate the pain of losses, if you should have that unfortunate experience. The government allows you to deduct a certain fixed amount of your investment losses for a particular year from your taxable income for that year. The current laws stipulate a maximum income tax deduction of $3,000 of cumulative investment losses. You can also apply the $3,000 in losses to capital gains you earned from other stocks. And, if you've lost more than $3,000 in a year, you can carry forward the remaining amount to be applied to next year's taxes. If you lost $5,000 this year in bad stock investments, you can deduct $3,000 from your tax bill this year, and you can deduct $2,000 of that loss next year.

Calculating the capital gain or loss on your investments is fairly straightforward if you have only done a small amount of investing. The more you buy and sell stocks in a given year, however, the greater the number of total transactions you have to consider when calculating your net gain or loss for the year, and the greater the complexity of figuring those numbers. If you bought 100 shares of Zza at $5 and sold those shares at $70, in 14 months, you'd have a long-term capital gain of $65 per share, or $6,500 total.

Amount of sale	minus	Purchase price	equals	Capital gain
$(100 \times 70 = 7,000)$	–	$(100 \times 5 = 500)$	=	$6,500

On the other hand, if you bought 100 shares of Zza at $70 and sold it in three months for $60, you'd have a short-term capital loss of $10 per share, or $1,000, that can be deducted from your taxable income for that year. Or you can use the $1,000 to offset other capital gains.

Amount of sale	minus	Purchase price	equals	Capital loss
$(100 \times 60 = 6,000)$	–	$(100 \times 70 = 7,000)$	=	$1,000

Suppose you bought 100 shares of Zza at $40, then later bought another 100 shares at $60, then sold all 200 shares in six months for $70. Your net gain for that year would be $4,000.

Amount of sale	minus	Purchase price	equals	Capital gain
$(100 \times 70 = 7,000)$	–	$(100 \times 40 = 4,000)$	=	$3,000
$(100 \times 70 = 7,000)$	–	$(100 \times 60 = 6,000)$	=	$1,000
Total capital gain:				$4,000

Calculating FIFO

Suppose you made the same purchases as above, 100 shares at $40 and later 100 shares at $60, then sold only 100 of those 200 shares that year when the stock price hit $70. To calculate your capital gain or loss for this scenario, you need to know about the FIFO, or first-in/first-out, formula. FIFO means that the capital gain or loss for these transactions must be computed based on whichever stock transaction occurred first. In this example, the capital gain you would be taxed on is $3,000:

Amount of sale	minus	Purchase price	equals	Capital gain
$(100 \times 70 = 7,000)$	–	$(100 \times 40 = 4,000)$	=	$3,000

Maybe you're thinking, "Why can't I be taxed based on the later transaction in which I paid more for the stock, so I don't have to pay as much tax this year?" The truth is that you can, but you have to be very specific about your intentions at the time you place the order with your broker to sell the stock. If you tell your broker to sell 100 shares of Zza at $70, you'll be taxed on the basis of the FIFO formula. If, however, you tell your broker to sell 100 shares of Zza at $70 versus the later purchase, you're instructing him to sell a specific group of shares that you own. In this case, the sell transaction will be based on the shares you bought at $60, and your tax liability for that year will be $1,000. But remember, if you don't arrange with your broker to sell specific shares, the FIFO method will be used to calculate your gain.

Amount of sale	minus	Purchase price	equals	Capital gain
$(100 \times 70 = 7,000)$	–	$(100 \times 60 = 6,000)$	=	$1,000

You can extrapolate from these examples just how much effort figuring out your tax liability will take for any particular year. The primary thing to remember is that you are

only liable when a sell transaction is actually executed. If you buy 100 shares of Zza stock at $5 and it shoots up to $70, you aren't liable for a $65 gain unless you sell the stock at $70. What you have in your hands at that point is a "paper gain," or an unrealized capital gain. Just as you wouldn't be able to buy that new car on an unrealized capital gain, but you sure could on an actual gain, your eccentric Uncle Sam is only going to come knocking when you realize your gains and have the cash in your hands.

The Regulators: Government's Involvement as Market Watchdog

While the stock market in America tends to operate on free-market principles, which allow trading to take place with little direct government involvement, the federal government has nonetheless enacted many regulations to control the way things are done in the markets. The purpose of these controls is not intentional interference with the wheels of commerce, however. The laws exist to check the abuses that inevitably arise in a marketplace where so much money is continuously at stake.

Many of the laws that govern the securities markets were enacted during the Great Depression. The period preceding the great stock market crash of 1929 was one in which the government had little regulatory involvement with the securities markets. After the crash, investigations discovered a number of abuses in the securities industry. Many companies issued stock that may have been worthless or that may have involved greater risk than most investors might have been able to absorb. The Securities Act of 1933 sought to protect small investors from scams and rip-offs. One of the primary results of the 1933 legislation was the requirement of the full disclosure statement that must always be issued before the initial public offering of a stock.

In 1934, the government created the Securities and Exchange Commission (SEC) and vested it with the power of enforcing the rules of the Act of 1933. The SEC not only enforces the requirement of the full disclosure statement, but it also attempts to ensure that investors are fully informed about the risks involved with investing and monitors market activity to prevent mishandling by corporations or brokers. The SEC also keeps track of insider trading—stock transactions conducted by employees or officers of the corporation. While insiders may legally buy and sell a company's stock, it is illegal for them to use their inside, nonpublic information to manipulate the market for their gain. The SEC maintains a comprehensive set of rules to which insiders must adhere when they buy and sell stock in their company.

Another regulatory agency that monitors market activity is the National Association of Securities Dealers (NASD), an association of brokers and dealer firms in the over-the-counter (OTC) market. While the NASD is not a government agency, it serves a purpose similar to the SEC: to protect the investor by ensuring quality of service, requiring full disclosure of pertinent information, and protecting against abuses.

Among the responsibilities of the NASD is the certification and registration of brokers. In fact, another, more official name for a broker is a "registered representative." This term refers to the fact that the representative has successfully passed the NASD's registration process. The representative must pass a strenuous examination that covers nearly every aspect of the securities markets to ensure that the broker is knowledgeable about the industry and qualified to offer investment advice. While these agencies cannot prevent absolutely all instances of abuse, they contribute greatly to making the securities markets a safer place for most investors.

Get Professional Help

The laws that govern taxation are complex and always changing, so if you are an active investor, you should think about getting professional help to handle your taxes. The cost of professional accounting services will probably far offset the headaches you might get by trying to do it all on your own. Of course, if you're willing to read through the tax documents and aren't afraid of number crunching, feel free to dive right in and figure those taxes yourself. The point is that investing can be both fun and profitable, but there are serious responsibilities involved and serious consequences for not following the rules.

If you have any doubt about your ability to figure out your taxes correctly, or if the sight of a "long form" makes your stomach churn, find yourself an accountant. You can find one in your neighborhood simply by opening up the Yellow Pages and looking in the "A" section. Call a few of them and ask some questions. Find out what they'll charge you to fill out your tax forms and do all the calculations for you. If the rates seem exorbitant or you don't feel comfortable with the person on the other end of the

phone, keep looking. You'll be paying good money for a valuable service, and you have the right to work with someone you feel you like and can trust.

If you decide to prepare your taxes yourself, make sure that you don't let yourself procrastinate until April 14th. The worst thing you can do is torture yourself by trying to do it all while you're under the gun. Get your papers together and start trying to figure things out as early as possible. This way, you'll get your responsibilities taken care of without losing all your hair in the process. And if you find you do need help, you'll still have enough time to get it.

IT'S
in the
NUMBERS

CHAPTER THREE

Are you ready to get into the real nitty-gritty of investing? If you've got a **fistful of dollars** *just burning to be invested and you're ready to get into the* **action,** *now you need to learn how to evaluate the* **companies** *whose stock you may be interested in buying.*

You could listen to what your broker tells you and just buy a few stocks without really knowing why, or you could take the advice of your brother-in-law who's been investing for years (even though he's never managed to make any money from his quixotic forays into the stock market "jungle," as he calls it). Or, you could read on and learn about the techniques used to determine the value of corporations and stocks and the tools that can help you make intelligent, informed investment decisions.

Regardless of what anyone tells you about foolproof investment strategies and surefire ways to make big bucks in the market, every investment you ever make in your life

from now until the end of your investing days is going to involve some measure of risk. There are no guarantees in the market. No matter how solid a company's track record, no matter how great its future prospects, no matter how many New York cabdrivers tell you it is the best thing since sliced bread, the fact is that the stock could go up, or the stock could go down.

Value Investing

There are techniques, though, that can help minimize the risk. One of these methods is called value investing, which relies on your willingness to study carefully the fundamentals of the companies you're considering investing in. The basic strategy of this system is to look at the underlying value of a corporation as the primary criterion for deciding whether or not to buy that company's stock. And the way to figure out a company's value is to study the numbers. With that in mind, this chapter will give you the basic math that you, as an investor, can learn to love and appreciate. This is the math that will help you on the way to becoming a successful investor.

The Balance Sheet

The first source of information you'll want to look at when you evaluate a company as a potential investment is the company's balance sheet. This document can tell you a tremendous amount about the financial health and well-being of a company, either enhancing your interest in the company's prospects or filling you with fear and loathing at the thought of ever putting a penny of your hard-earned cash into that sinking ship of an organization. The balance sheet will give you a good indication of whether the company is successfully performing the great balancing act between positive and negative cash flow. If you think of a company as walking a tightrope between expenses and income (perhaps much like your own financial situation), you can think of the balance sheet as the television crew that lets the whole country watch this performance from the edge of their seats.

Two primary sections of information on a balance sheet are crucial to investors: assets and liabilities. Take a look at the balance sheet for Nellie's Nummy Nuggets, an imaginary potato dumpling manufacturer based in Peoria, Illinois:

	2001	2000
Current Assets		
Cash and equivalents	$ 5,000,000	$3,500,000
Accounts receivable	500,000	2,000,000
Inventories	4,500,000	1,000,000
Total Current Assets	10,000,000	6,500,000
Property, plant, and equipment	$ 7,500,000	$4,000,000
Less accumulated depreciation	1,000,000	750,000
Net property	6,500,000	3,250,000
Total Assets	16,500,000	9,750,000
Current Liabilities		
Accounts payable	$ 2,500,000	$1,200,000
Accrued expenses	3,500,000	2,300,000
Total Current Liabilities	6,000,000	3,500,000
Long-Term Debt	$ 750,000	$1,250,000
Shareholders' Equity		
Common stock, $1 par value	$ 7,000,000	$4,000,000
Retained earnings	2,750,000	1,000,000
Total Liabilities, Debt, and		
Shareholders' Equity	16,500,000	9,750,000

The information runs from top to bottom in two columns. The number of columns displayed depends on how long the company has been in existence as well as how much history the company wants to show on the current report; some companies only display one column for the current year, while others will have ten columns. This comparative earnings history of the company helps you determine how the company is doing not only now, but also in relation to previous years. The current year's numbers are not even necessarily the most critical figures. What investors are most interested in is the trend indicated by the differences between years. You study a balance sheet to see if the company is on a positive growth pattern and if it's keeping its expenses

OTHER FINANCIAL DOCUMENTS AND TOOLS

While the balance sheet and income statement will be your primary sources of information on a company's financial health and well-being, other sources can provide a great deal of useful knowledge about a company. These come from the company as well as from outside sources.

The **statement of cash** flows is offered by the company and gives investors a different view of the company's financial condition. It provides information about specific inflows and outflows of cash that the company has experienced over a certain period of time.

in check. You're also looking for clues to the company's cash flow as well as its debt versus cash situation. Here are the main points to consider on any balance sheet, from the top down.

Cash and Equivalents

This is perhaps the most important line on the balance sheet. If the cash position of a company is positive, then you have an almost instantaneous indication that the company's cash flow situation is probably healthy. Lots of cash is the most valuable asset for a company to have for a number of reasons. If you make that direct parallel to your own financial situation, you can see why. First of all, cash is the raison d'être of the business itself. Unless you're looking at a not-for-profit organization (and you're probably not, because you're reading a book about how to make money in the stock market!), you're looking at a corporation, and corporations exist to make profits. Although a positive cash line is definitely a good indicator, a negative cash line is not necessarily a bad one. Different kinds of companies can have a small or large amount of cash on hand, and that may or may not be a good indicator of whether or not the company is a good investment. Take a look at cash, but don't stop there.

There are, of course, many other benefits that a successful company creates for society, like jobs and community stability, but companies generally don't place these benefits at the top of the list of primary corporate goals. It's the bottom line that ultimately determines if the company even continues to survive, let alone produce those social benefits. Once a corporation has sufficient cash to pay the bills, salaries, taxes, and other expenses and still stay afloat, it's well on its way to being a stable, solid company.

Another reason to get excited about a company with a good deal of cash is that a cash-rich company will have less trouble staying in business if it experiences a temporary short-fall in sales or revenues. Suppose Nellie discovers that her nuggets are particularly hot sellers in the winter, when people are looking for more hearty fare to stick to their cold ribs. During the summer slump, however, Nellie still has a payroll and a factory to maintain, a number of large freezers to keep running (where she stores those nummy nuggets before shipment), and a host of other fixed costs she has to keep up with. It doesn't take a mathematical genius to figure out what would happen to Nellie's cash flow situation during those slow months, if her business had to rely solely on its revenue stream from sales to pay those bills. If Nellie has a large and consistent cash position, she'll be able to get through those difficult months without any trouble at all. But if the cash isn't there, she can only put off her creditors for so long before they'll start making her life difficult.

Another way to determine the stability of a stock is to evaluate the company's cash position per share. In Nellie's case, the company has seven million shares outstanding, and according to the company's balance sheet, the company has $5 million cash on hand. Dividing $5 million by seven million shares gives us a cash value for the company of $.71 per share.

One way to look at this is that no matter how bad the market for potato dumplings becomes, Nellie's value per share isn't going to drop below $.71 per share. How do we know this? Well, if Nellie's goes out of business, unless the company is burning that cash like the old '71 El Dorado in Nellie's garage burns gas, at least 71 pennies per share of real live money will be available for distribution to creditors and shareholders.

For the company that burns dollar bills to fuel its building's heating system, its stock can quite pos-

FINANCIAL DOCUMENTS

Annual Report. The corporate annual report is usually something of an imposing tome meant to give investors the big picture of what the company has been up to. This report usually contains the balance sheet, income statement, and statement of cash flows, but it also offers plain English discussions about the business from the perspective of its management team. While this information is softer than the pure numbers, you can still learn a good deal about business from these discussions.

sibly drop below the company's cash per share amount, but these circumstances are rare. The stock would drop below the current cash position in this situation, because future projections assume that the cash will rapidly dwindle down to nothing. Key point to all this: Cash is good.

Accounts Receivable and Inventories

While the balance sheet lists these as assets, and strictly speaking they are exactly that, you have to look at these items with a bit of skepticism. Accounts receivable are dollars that the company has not yet received from its customers for the purchase of goods or services. In Nellie's case, the accounts receivable would probably include money that came from sales to restaurants that were serving her dumplings. Now the restaurant business is a slippery fish indeed, and restaurants are notorious for going out of business in the blink of an eye. If Nellie's balance sheet shows huge amounts of receivables, your first reaction might be to get excited because receivables are decent indicators of sales. However, those dollars have not yet been converted to cash, which is liquid and spendable. Nellie isn't going to open her new manufacturing plant on the basis of a large amount of receivables, but she might if she had lots of cash.

While the difference may be subtle, it is very important. If Nellie's biggest customer happens to be Zza (Joe has expanded the business again, this time to include salads and dumplings!), but they happen to be going through some financial strain at the time, Nellie may never see those receivables converted to cash, and that could ultimately result in a big write-off, which would adversely affect the bottom line next year or the year after that.

Inventories, too, are a kind of asset, but unlike receivables that reflect sales and have a decent chance of getting converted to cash, inventories are assets that are sitting somewhere in a warehouse waiting to be bought. A company that makes and sells a product, like dumplings for example, needs to maintain a certain level of inventory to be able to fill orders. But if the level of inventory on the balance sheet is very high in comparison to cash and receivables, you might be looking at an indicator that the company is having a hard time unloading its goods into the marketplace. If nobody wants to eat Nellie's dumplings, she's eventually going to wind up with a warehouse full of rotten dough that has to be thrown away at a loss. The goal of the company is to convert

those inventories into sales. The sales will then go to the receivables line of the balance sheet (unless they were cash sales) and then finally end up as cash, if all goes well. Keep an eye on inventories and receivables as they change from year to year. If you see these numbers decreasing, with cash increasing, you'll know you're looking at a good potential investment.

Net Property

This line of the balance sheet is derived from subtracting accumulated depreciation (based on historical costs) from the property, plant, and equipment line. Property is another of those tricky assets that look good on paper but may in fact be little more than a liability in disguise. This kind of asset is even harder to convert to cash than receivables or inventories, and determining exactly how much value exists in a piece of land or a manufacturing plant can be difficult. If Nellie's company runs short of operating capital (cash), it's not going to be able to convert its property, plant, and equipment into cash to keep things running along. If Nellie sells her plant, she won't be able to make any more dumplings! Of course, she could lease the space from its new owner, but then the lease would become part of the ongoing cost of running the business and would negatively impact the bottom line.

If Nellie goes out of business, however, the sale of property might help pay creditors and shareholders and so could prove to be a very valuable asset. But its value depends on whether a buyer wants a dumpling manufacturing plant in Peoria. If the economy is in a slump, Nellie might have trouble unloading the property, and it would be little more than a millstone around the neck of the failed company. You don't want to have to drive through Peoria, point your finger at the abandoned buildings up for auction, and tell your friends how you made that investment because you thought the balance sheet looked great with all those property assets!

FINANCIAL DOCUMENTS

Digest of Earnings Report. This report is usually available in the financial press when companies issue their quarterly earnings statements. Here you'll find a breakdown of the company's revenues, net income, number of shares outstanding, and earnings per share for the current quarter, as well as for the same quarter of last year.

Accumulated depreciation is one of those unfortunate facts of life that nobody really likes to think about too much. Depreciation is what happens to just about anything you buy, other than perhaps property. While the value of Nellie's property (defined here as land and buildings) may increase in value if the location is good and the economy is stable, the value of Nellie's refrigerators and dough-mixing machines will never do anything but decrease in value over time. When a company buys equipment, it has to determine a period of time over which to depreciate the value of that equipment. So if Nellie buys five new, huge, commercial dumpling refrigerators, she has to determine how long she thinks she'll get value out of those things before she has to upgrade to new equipment again. If the average life of one of those refrigerators is five years, and it costs $50,000 to buy, Nellie is going to deduct $10,000 per year as depreciation for each of those monsters. That affects the bottom line and is therefore subtracted from the value of property, plant, and equipment as a whole. Depreciation is unavoidable and shouldn't scare you away from an investment unless it becomes a ridiculously large amount. If, for example, Nellie had to abandon a plant because sales were down and she couldn't sell that plant, you'd see a pretty huge impact on the bottom line. This much depreciation would clearly indicate problems and give you a clue to stay away from this investment.

So how does Nellie's current balance sheet stack up in the assets area? You can see that her cash position has increased from $3,500,000 to $5,000,000 from 2000 to 2001, a good sign. Nellie must be doing a decent amount of business to be able to sock away extra cash, and cash is very desirable. Her accounts receivable have dropped from $2,000,000 to $500,000 over that year. This looks like a positive sign, because it probably indicates that her customers are paying their bills and not just accumulating credit. However, inventories have increased from $1,000,000 to $4,500,000 from one year to the next. This red flag should prompt you to find out more. Is Nellie increasing inventory because she anticipates a great year ahead and needs to have more stock on hand to sell? Or did she overestimate her sales for last year? If these inventories are the result of slacking sales, she may have to write these off next year. Also, the decrease in accounts receivable could indicate that business has been slow, despite the increase in cash shown on the balance sheet. Maybe Nellie's cash position has increased because she sold more stock to generate cash to compensate for a drop in sales.

Farther down the balance sheet, you'll see that shareholders's equity has grown, indicating that she may have issued more stock. Nellie's property, plant, and equipment has increased in 2001 as well, indicating that her company invested in some new equipment or a new building. You'll have to dig around a bit to see if these expenses are justified by sales or whether she is mismanaging the company. When you start analyzing the income statement a little later, it will answer most of these questions for you. For now, the balance sheet seems pretty positive overall. As long as the company's cash position is solid, it should be able to survive a period of slower sales.

Current Liabilities: Accounts Payable and Accrued Expenses

Now it's time to take a look at the bottom half of the balance sheet, which describes the company's liabilities. The first liability you'll see is accounts payable. This refers to dollars that the company owes to other companies for things like supplies, materials, equipment, and services. Nellie needs to buy flour and spices to mix, and she needs to ship those nuggets out to the market via rail or truck or some other delivery mechanism. Generally, businesses don't pay for these things with cash but rather use their credit lines to get what they need. Using credit can help a company balance its cash flow because its customers are probably paying for dumplings on credit as well, but it adds dollars to the short-term liability the company is responsible for. You can't always consider a high amount of

WHAT IS THE OLDEST COMPANY LISTED ON THE NEW YORK STOCK EXCHANGE?

Well, oldest can mean a number of different things. For example, in 1791 **the Bank of New York** became the first corporate stock to be traded in New York City. Although the bank is still traded on the NYSE today, it has not been listed continuously on the exchange.

The **Consolidated Edison Company of New York** is the stock that has the distinction of being the longest continuously listed stock. Con Edison first traded on the NYSE in 1824 under the name New York Gas Light Company.

Finally, the **Dexter Corporation,** which was first listed in 1968, was founded in 1767, making it the oldest company in terms of its own longevity.

accounts payable as a bad sign because—and you can see this from Nellie's balance sheet—sometimes the credit is used to beef up inventories for an anticipated increase in sales. As long as the company has positive cash flow, it can pay these off in short order.

Then there are the accrued expenses, which include things like salaries paid to employees. These, like accounts payable, are typically short-term expenses. Your main concern about these current liabilities is that the company is acting responsibly and paying its expenses on time and in good order. If your research indicates that these liabilities keep adding up without getting paid, the company may be in danger of getting sued for nonpayment of debts or for breach of contract. You want to make sure the company is keeping its creditors and employees happy; otherwise it will eventually run out of both.

Long-Term Debt

This category is probably a more important indicator than the current liabilities (accounts payable and accrued expenses). If the company has a large amount of long-term debt and that amount grows each year, the company is probably experiencing cash flow problems. Long-term debt is usually the result of borrowing to purchase large items like equipment or property. It also includes any bonds issued by the company to help finance operations or large purchases. If the long-term debt grows consistently without a corresponding increase in revenues and cash, the company is relying too heavily on borrowed money to keep itself in business. Ultimately, a great deal of long-term debt, coupled with problems paying current liabilities and a lack of growth in cash, will cause the business to fold. Again, think of your own finances. If your credit card debts are so large that all your income is going to pay off your creditors, you'll eventually wind up bankrupt, because sooner or later people are going to figure out that you're living on borrowed money. One day, your sources of credit will dry up, and you'll be forced to find some other way of getting by.

Keep a close eye on a company's long-term debt over time. If, as in Nellie's case, the number shrinks year after year, it means that the company is reducing its debt regularly. If the number keeps growing, you'll have to find out why and decide whether or not you think the company is going to be able to pay off that debt before going out of business. Be very wary of companies with consistently large amounts of debt, and don't hesitate to avoid buying stock in an otherwise attractive company if its debt is out of control.

Shareholders' Equity and Retained Earnings

Shareholders' equity refers to the amount of stock outstanding. If the number keeps rising, it might be cause for concern, because while it is common for companies to issue additional stock at times to generate necessary cash for operations, generating cash flow from sales is far preferable than stock offerings. In addition, as more shares are poured into the marketplace, the value of existing shares tends to go down because the stock becomes easier to acquire. Imagine, for example, a company with only 1 million shares of stock outstanding, as opposed to a company with 50 million shares outstanding. If both companies are successful, the one with fewer shares will probably experience greater price appreciation. This is simply an expression of the law of supply and demand; as demand for something increases without an equivalent increase in supply, the price will rise. If the company you're considering issues lots of shares just to keep itself in business, you might reconsider whether to buy that stock. As more shares flood the market, your initial stake will depreciate in value.

Retained earnings refers to money the company has earned from sales that it has decided to reinvest back into the business before paying out any dividends it may have declared. Small, growing companies usually won't be paying out dividends to their shareholders, so unless the money is going toward increasing the company's cash position, it will be invested into growing the business. This figure can be considered a positive item, even though it's listed in the liabilities section. If you see a large amount of retained earnings along with a good cash position and low expenses and debt, you're looking at a company that is managing cash efficiently by using its earnings to expand its business without having to borrow money. You actually want to see the company invest in itself. Think about it: if the company doesn't believe in itself enough to invest in itself, why should you believe in that company? As long as this money is retained for growth and improvement of the business, you generally have nothing to worry about.

Company Valuation

Does the Market Ever Overvalue or Undervalue a Company?

Many investors are adherents of the efficient market hypothesis, which says that the markets are efficient in pricing securities because all the expectations and knowledge of all investors in the market have come to bear on a stock's price. This makes each stock's price its "fair value" at any given time. While this concept may prove to be true for individual stocks over long periods of time, equally convincing arguments claim that the markets are highly inefficient due to the great number of investors with wildly diverging approaches to managing their money. If you've spent any time watching the movement of stock prices, you're bound to notice that sometimes stock prices rise or fall dramatically based on those generally insignificant tidbits of noninformation known as rumors. Other times, stock prices will skyrocket on expectations of future growth, even if a company has no past track record to justify that expectation. All sorts of anomalies occur in the markets on a daily basis, and if you're able to keep your eyes wide open, you can use them to your advantage.

If you find a company, for example, that your research indicates to be a solid and well-managed organization, but the stock price seems low, you may want to explore this phenomenon. The company may have had a bad quarter, rumors may be flying, or it may be stuck in an out-of-favor sector, but if you know that the company is solid, you may have found a winner.

Take Ross Stores (ROST), for example. Retail just ain't cool, at least not next to the eBays and Yahoo!s of the world. But Ross Dress for Less, the second largest discount apparel retailer in the country, could be a silk dress at a T-shirt price. In the first half of 2000, the company reported sales figures that didn't meet projections. Couple that with an anticipated economic slowdown, and the stock dropped 30% in a month—from $24 to $16. This price drop may be a blessing in disguise for bargain hunters. Ross's has demonstrated steady growth over the last five years (compounding 14.4% since 1995), the management team is stable and seasoned, and they plan to continue their growth with new stores and expanding merchandise lines. Based on Ross's historical performance and sound growth strategies, 20-25% returns are likely in the next five years—a projection many investors might find inviting.

Putting It All Together

Looking over Nellie's balance sheet as a whole, we see a company that seems pretty strong and on the right track. The company's cash has grown, while receivables have shrunk. Although inventories and property have increased significantly, these may be indications that the company is gearing up for some serious sales growth. You may have to do some additional research to figure out what the economy is doing and whether you can see any trends that would lead you to believe that dumpling sales are about to blast off. But it's good to see that Nellie's total assets have increased over the past year.

As far as the company's liabilities go, you can see that accounts payable and accrued expenses have increased, but this may be a sign of good financial management on the part of the company. If Nellie can keep more cash on hand and pay off her creditors slowly, she'll be able to use the cash in her bank account more wisely by investing it and earning interest or by expanding her business. Long-term debt has dropped significantly, so you don't have much to worry about there. And while additional stock has been issued, it seems that the money was put to good use by increasing cash, paying down debt, and investing in the business.

Income Statement

The balance sheet for Nellie's Nummy Nuggets looks pretty good, but you're still missing some key pieces of information. You can make a few assumptions about sales and revenues from the balance sheet, but you can't be sure, for example, whether the increase in Nellie's cash situation is the result of a growth in sales or simply the effect of selling additional stock or other assets such as property. This is where the rubber meets the road: if the balance sheet has lots of pretty numbers, but they've all been generated by selling shares of stock rather than by increasing sales, the company may be nothing but a nice smoke and mirrors magic show. The income statement, also known as the profit and loss statement, or P&L, is where you'll get the answers to fill in the blanks left by the balance sheet. While the balance sheet can give you a solid look at a company's financial position at the end of the year, the income statement is where you'll learn about the company's cash flow. You'll also be able to glean information such as the company's profit margin, its net income, its expense ratio, and its earnings per share. Let's take a look at the income statement for Nellie's Nummy Nuggets and figure out if we like what we see:

	2001	2000
Profit		
Revenue	$17,500,000	$12,000,000
Cost of sales	7,000,000	5,000,000
Gross profit	10,500,000	7,000,000
Operating Expenses		
Selling, general, and administrative expenses	$ 3,500,000	$ 3,000,000
Research and development	500,000	350,000
Total operating expenses	4,000,000	3,350,000
Net Income		
Before taxes	$ 6,500,000	$ 4,650,000
Income taxes	2,145,000	1,534,500
After taxes	4,355,000	3,115,500
Shares outstanding	7,000,000	4,000,000
Earnings per share	$ 0.62	$ 0.78

Revenue and Net Income

The top of the income statement shows you the total dollar amount of sales the company has pulled in for the period of the report. You're always looking for an increase here, regardless of anything else that may be going on with the company. Growth in revenues means growth in business, no two ways about it. On the other hand, if you only look at revenue growth without considering things like cost of sales; selling, general, and administrative expenses; or income taxes; you're not going to get a clear picture of the company's financial condition. Again, consider your own finances. If you're pulling in $100,000 a year, but spending $95,000 on rent and car payments, you aren't going to have anything left for your savings account, for going out to the movies, or for silly stuff like food and beer. If the total inflow of dollars on a company's P&L looks wonderful, but those dollars are being misspent or mismanaged, you'll have to reconsider your investment. Net income is by far a better indicator of a company's real financial situation because it takes expenditures into account, but revenue

growth from year to year is where you'll learn about the company's success (or lack thereof) in selling its products or services.

Earnings per Share

The earnings per share (EPS) is the most widely used and significant measure of a company's profitability and success. You can calculate this yourself easily by dividing net income by shares outstanding. In Nellie's case for 2001, this comes to: $4,355,000 ÷ 7,000,000 = $.62. When investors talk about the bottom line, they're talking about this number. Stocks are typically priced in relation to earnings per share, so the higher the EPS, the higher the stock's price will be. Your goal as an investor is to find companies that consistently show increasing earnings per share, year after year after year. These companies will reward you with the capital gains that make investing exciting and profitable.

After seeing Nellie's EPS decrease from $.78 per share to $.62 per share between 2000 and 2001, you may be tempted to raise an eyebrow at Nellie's stock. And well you should! The rest of the market probably reacted the same way after this earnings announcement was released, and the stock most likely dropped in price. You may be wondering why the stock would drop, considering that revenues increased 46 percent from $12 million to $17.5 million over that same year. The clue to answer this lies in the line just above the EPS on the

FINANCIAL DOCUMENTS

Corporate Dividend News. Another report that you'll find in the financial press, the dividend news report, provides information on newly declared dividends by companies, changes to existing dividends, and dividend information about companies that have had stock splits.

The Value Line Investment Survey. The *Value Line Investment Survey* is one of the most popular and respected investment tools available. While the cost of subscribing can be expensive, most public libraries have copies. *The Value Line* analyzes stocks from a variety of perspectives and provides a comprehensive source of information about the financials of companies they track.

income statement. The reason earnings per share dropped despite an increase in revenues is that the company almost doubled the total number of shares outstanding from four million to seven million. You saw this increase in shares on the balance sheet

FINANCIAL DOCUMENTS

The 10-Q Statement and Other SEC Documents.

The company's quarterly report (10-Q) is filed with the SEC within 90 days of the close of the fiscal quarter. The company provides a detailed analysis of its quarterly financial condition. While in the past accessing these documents was difficult, with the advent of electronic communications like the Internet, you can now view 10-Q statements almost immediately when they're filed, if the company used the SEC's electronic filing program. This program will soon be required of all companies, so you'd be well advised to keep a bookmark to the SEC's Web site on your browser. The URL for the SEC is <www.sec.gov>.

under shareholders's equity, and now you know why it is a negative indicator for investors.

When the number of shares increases, the EPS generally drops in reaction to the increase in shares, unless the company has experienced a miraculous increase in revenues, which would offset this effect. This effect is called dilution of a stock's value. The more shares outstanding, the harder it is for the company to have high earnings per share. And the lower the EPS, generally the lower the stock's value.

At this point, you should try to discover just why Nellie's Nummy Nuggets decided to issue another three million shares of stock. You can try to contact the company, or you can dig through the annual report to find out the reason for the additional offering, and you may or may not find what you're looking for. If the company is carefully avoiding answering your questions, consider finding another investment. You're in this to try to maximize your returns by coming to intelligent and informed conclusions. If you can't get the information you need, move on.

If you find out the reason for the stock offering, you'll have to decide whether you think that offering was justified and whether you're still willing to hang on to that stock. If Nellie's sales and income were down and she sold shares just to drum up some additional cash, it's time for you to seek other opportunities. On the other hand, if Nellie sold more stock to generate cash for a major expansion into a new market niche, you may want to hang on despite the market's negative reaction to the drop in EPS.

Profit Margin

This figure will help you determine whether to keep the stock in the face of an additional stock offering, like Nellie's recently had. The profit margin is the net income divided by the revenue. Margins should show steady, positive signs of growth. At the very least, they should remain consistent over time. If margins decline, you need to ask more questions: is this a one-time drop due to an expansion of business, or is this the result of poor money management? When margins grow, they reflect solid financial management on the part of the company, because growing margins show a good level of control over the costs involved in running the business. If margins decline, you may be looking at a company with sloppy money managers at the helm. It just might be time to jump ship.

Comparing Nellie's profit margin between 2000 and 2001, you'll see an amazingly high margin each year, which should immediately warm your heart. However, there's a slight dip in the margin in 2001. The margin for 2000 was an incredible 25.9 percent ($3,115,500 ÷ $12,000,000 × 100 = 25.9%), but in 2001 Nellie's margin lost one percentage point ($4,355,000 ÷ $17,500,000 = 24.9%). Now, 1 percent of a margin this high may not be much to get nervous about, but the fact is that not only has the company's profit margin declined, but its number of shares has dramatically increased, and its earnings per share have decreased. This may be a clue that the business is not handling its growth very well, or that management has gotten a bit lax. Then again, it may just indicate that the company's margins are getting more in line with the rest of the dumpling industry. Perhaps Nellie's margins were unusually high in her first year of business, and now they're settling into a more common level. You'll have to do some more homework to find out, and you'll definitely want to keep an eye on this company's numbers as time rolls on.

STOCK TECH

These are some of the major **technological advances** that have affected the stock markets.

1928—Quotation bureau established

1953—First automated quotation service in use

1962—First optical card readers

Expense Ratio

The expense ratio is another way of evaluating the deftness of a company's money management skills. This figure is calculated in a manner similar to the profit margin, except that it compares revenues to expenses rather than to net profits. You figure the expense ratio by dividing the expenses on the income statement by the revenues, so for Nellie's, the expense ratio would be 63 percent:

$7,000,000 + $3,500,000 + $500,000 = $11,000,000
$11,000,000 ÷ $17,500,000 = .63
.63 × 100 = 63%

Believe it or not, a 63 percent expense ratio is not bad for most companies, but you have to take into account how the company's expense ratio compares to that of other companies in the same or a similar industry. If most dumpling manufacturers have expense ratios of 50 percent, and Nellie's is way up there at 63 percent, the company may be spending too much money. However, Nellie's expense ratio and profit margin are among the best to be seen anywhere in the corporate world. On these merits, Nellie's Nummy Nuggets looks like a pretty profitable enterprise.

Research and development (R&D) play a big role in a company's expenses. Depending on the company's line of business, research and development investments could make the difference between success or failure over the long term. For a company that produces dumplings by the ton, R&D might be a moot point. However, when you consider that food-related industries are often highly susceptible to trends and changes in taste, Nellie's best interests may lie in doing little market research to determine what the most popular new dumplings might be. This research might also involve the development of new varieties of dumplings that can be sampled by groups of taste testers. If the company is in a business area where R&D might make a difference over the long term, make sure its income statement doesn't show a significant drop here. While the short-term expense savings might produce a nice effect on the bottom line for a year or two, the lack of development will eventually catch up with the company when its competitors blow it out of the water with their new and improved smoked-jalapeño-pineapple instant dumplings. Keeping up with industry trends and market sentiments helps turn a business into a long-term successful venture. Nellie's Nummy

Nuggets increased its R&D expense from $350,000 to $500,000, so it's clear that the company's management understands the value of research and development.

Hi-Low-Close: How to Read a Stock Table

Now that you've gotten a taste of some of the gritty parts of investing, get yourself a glass of water, wash that grit out of your mouth, and sit right back down on that hot sand. The stock market is driven by lots of numbers, and as you've probably realized by now, you won't be able to make decent (or winning!) investment decisions simply by pulling a stock symbol out of a hat. You can't build that sand castle of your dreams just by pouring over a company's annual report statistics, although that is most certainly a great place to start. Once you've gotten a handle on the company's financial situation, you're going to want to watch the stock's performance for a while to see if your guesses about its direction are even remotely on target. You'll also need to study the history of the stock price over time to see if you can spot any historical trends that might help you make better investment decisions. To watch a stock's performance over time, you need to understand how to read stock prices as they're quoted in the papers and in charts from various sources.

For example, when you open *The Wall Street Journal* to the financial pages and turn to the stock quotes section, you'll see something that looks like this, with hundreds of rows of information, each pertaining to a particular stock:

52 Weeks				Yld		Vol				Net	
Hi	Lo	Stock	Sym	Div	%	PE	100s	Hi	Lo	Close	Chg
143	109	ZzaInc	ZZA	1.40	1.0	23	850	143	138	140	–2

This is a stock table. It's where you'll get most of your periodic updates on the prices and trading volume of your stocks. In this example, you're looking at the row for Zza, buried among all the other quotes listed for the day. The stock table seems cryptic the first few times you look at it, but once you get familiar with its format, you'll have no trouble finding the information you want. Here's a breakdown of the information contained on the table.

WHAT A SPREAD!

The Dow Jones Industrial Average has certainly had its ups and downs over the years. While the average typically inches upward over time, in 1996 the Dow's record high was broken countless times, with the average increasing by over 1,000 points that year. The **record high** of the Dow as of this writing was 11,722.98, which was achieved on January 14, 2000. The record low of the Dow average was 28.48, which occurred at the market's close on August 8, 1896.

52 Weeks—Hi Lo

The two columns under this general heading give you the highest and lowest closing prices recorded for that stock over the past year. This number can provide you with a good sense of the volatility, or the stability, of a stock's price over time. If the Hi and Lo numbers are far apart, they tell you that the stock is highly volatile and perhaps more risky. However, a more volatile stock also has more potential to make you money in a short period of time, because price swings tend to happen more quickly and in larger degrees. If you happen to see a little arrow just to the left of the Hi column, you'll know that the price has just reached either a new high or new low, depending on whether the arrow is pointing up or down.

Stock

This column simply, or not so simply, lists the name of the company. However, you'll soon learn that the name of the company as you know it does not always match the name shown in this column. Typically, unless the company's name is rather short and concise, you'll see an abbreviated version, which gets as much of the full name as possible into the column. In the above example, you can see that the stock name is listed as ZzaInc rather than Zza. Companies with larger names get even more interesting treatment. You'll get used to figuring out the truncated versions as you pour over these prices day after day.

Sym

This column lists the symbol that is used to trade the stock on the exchange or in the OTC or Nasdaq market. Every traded stock is issued a short symbol comprised of anywhere from one to five letters, which makes it easier for traders to keep track of lots of companies. Sometimes the symbols are obvious, as in the case of ZZA, but more often

than not they are cryptic, and you'll have to do a bit of research to determine the symbol of your favorite company.

One of the easiest ways to find out which stock symbols belong to what companies is to call your broker and ask. Another good way to find this information is to use the Internet or an online service like America Online or CompuServe. The World Wide Web stock market sites and forums all offer lookup utilities that can help you find the symbol for your company. Finally, you can call the company itself.

Div

This column displays the annual dividend per share, if any, that is paid by the company on a quarterly basis. For example, if you owned 100 shares of Zza, your dividend would be $1.40 per share per year ($140), paid out in quarterly installments of $35. This column is an estimated dividend based on the currently declared dividend and any relevant historical information. Companies can change the declared dividend amount if they choose to do so. If you see a stock in a table that lists a dividend, usually that stock will be less volatile and more stable than stocks that don't pay a dividend, because companies usually don't pay dividends unless they've become pretty well established.

Yld

This figure lists the dividend amount paid by the stock as a percentage of the current price of that stock. For Zza, the Yield is 1.0%, which you can calculate by dividing the dividend amount by the current price and then multiplying by 100 ($1.40 ÷ $140 × 100 = 1.0%). The yield is sometimes used as a measure of a stock's value because many

DIVIDENDS AND CAPITAL APPRECIATION: WHICH IS MORE IMPORTANT?

No one can tell you which is more important, because it all depends on what you are trying to get back from your investments. Just about anyone would be thrilled to double or triple their money in a matter of a few months or years. But the kinds of investments that offer those types of smashing returns usually carry higher risk. You have to ask yourself two fundamental questions before you invest in anything: (1) How much can I afford to lose? and (2) How much do I need to make?

investors are just as interested (if not more interested) in receiving dividends as they are in experiencing a capital gain.

PE

The price-to-earnings ratio, or the PE ratio, is the most widely used measure of a stock's value in the marketplace. Many other methods can be used to measure a stock's worth. One measure is the market price, which is determined by perceptions of a stock's value by traders and investors. The PE ratio is one measure that is often thought to pertain to the intrinsic value of a stock. It is calculated by dividing the current share price of the stock by the earnings per share of the company at the most recent annual announcement of those earnings. So, for Zza, which recently reported earnings of $6.10 per share (you'd get the EPS from the company's earnings release, or from a financial paper like *The Wall Street Journal*), the price-to-earnings ratio is 23 ($140 ÷ $6.10 = 23).

Generally speaking, the lower the PE ratio, the less risky the investment. Because the market is almost always willing to pay a premium for a good, solid company, if you can find such a creature with a low PE ratio to boot, you may have stumbled upon a great prospect. If the company is currently undervalued, it is usually just a matter of time before the market catches up and lifts the price of that company's stock. However, while the PE ratio is related to a company's intrinsic value, it is not actually a direct measure of the intrinsic worth of a company but is based in part on the market's perception of that company's value. Riskier companies with tremendous growth prospects may trade at higher PE ratios because the market expects their financial performance to continue to improve. Be careful: You can find plenty of low PE ratio stocks that stay cheap forever because the companies have dismal growth prospects.

When thinking about what a company is worth, you might try to imagine what the company as a whole would fetch for a seller on the open market if it were a simple, easy-to-unload commodity. A buyer would obviously pay a higher premium for a company that already had good earnings and was expected to grow significantly, because they would expect to achieve greater returns in the long run. In the same way, the PE ratio, while a good indicator of the company's value, must be interpreted differently for different companies because of their anticipated growth. A company that has had decent and consistent earnings year after year may settle into a PE ratio of ten, which is considered rather low. The PE ratio is low not because the company is in trouble or because people are bored with its consistent earnings, but because it has become stable and predictable and is not expected to grow much in the future. Another company that has experienced 75 percent increases in profit quarter after quarter over the past few years might be expected to continue that performance, and its PE ratio might be as high as 75.

So a low PE ratio is only a useful indicator in conjunction with other information that might lead you to believe that the company is underpriced by the market in comparison to similar companies in the same field. There are plenty of companies that are overpriced at PE ratios of 10, while other companies are underpriced at PE ratios of 75. A company that has steadily lost money and survives day-to-day on loans and new stock offerings will likely have a low PE ratio, because the market won't put a value on the company that is higher than its earnings. But the company with a PE ratio of 75 that keeps raking in money may still rise in price because of the market's expectation of that company's future growth. So while the PE ratio is a very useful number to consider, you have to know the whole story behind a company to know whether the PE ratio is too high or too low. The number by itself won't tell you anything more than that the market assumes the company as a salable commodity is worth its earnings multiplied by the PE ratio. The market has been wrong before, and if you can find a stock with a low PE ratio that should have a higher value based on other factors, you may have found a winner.

Vol 100s

The volume indicates the number of shares of a particular stock that traded that day. The table on page 69 indicates that 85,000 shares of Zza changed hands. This number seems fairly innocuous but may in fact contain a great deal of useful information for an investor. The trading volume of the stock tells you how much interest the market has in that particular investment. Now you may be thinking, "Who cares what the market thinks?" But the fact is that what the market thinks should mean a great deal to you. If, for example, your favorite company's stock is thinly traded, meaning that there is very little volume on a day-to-day basis, you may find yourself unable to unload that stock when it comes time for you to sell it. There's nothing more uncomfortable than trying to sell a stock as its price slowly sinks and finding that no one is out there to buy it.

Current versus Anticipated EPS

How a Short-Term "Loser" Can Have a High Stock Price

Most stocks are priced on the basis of earnings per share. But sometimes you'll run into stocks that are trading at such ridiculously high multiples of the company's earnings per share that you're bound to scratch your head in complete and utter amazement. You may even encounter stocks in the higher realms of stock valuations of companies that have consistently lost money.

Most growth stocks are valued less on the basis of current earnings per share as on anticipated earnings per share. If a new startup in an exciting and potentially very profitable industry catches the attention of the market, you may see its stock price rise astronomically on the expectation that the company will make a killing in its chosen field. The "Internet Gold Rush" of the 1990s gives a number of great examples of this kind of marketing reasoning. Witness companies such as Netscape and Amazon.com whose stocks quadrupled within a year after their initial public offerings. They enjoyed a market capitalization of billions of dollars long before they dreamed of turning a profit.

The marketplace anticipated that Netscape and Amazon.com would be dominant players in the exploding Internet industry, and therefore their stocks were in very high demand. These kinds of stocks can be very dangerous to investors because little value sustains the high stock price amid much speculation about the company's bright and glorious future that may never come to pass.

Another reason trading volume is important is that it may indicate future price movements. When a significant volume of stock changes hands on a regular basis and the stock's price continues to rise, you're looking at a high demand for that stock. The law of supply and demand tells you that when demand is high for something that is limited in quantity, the price tends to rise. When a large volume of stock trades faithfully with a rising price, you might consider investing because the trend indicates that the price will probably keep climbing for a while. The opposite is true, as well, so keep your eyes open to volume and price, as they go hand in hand. If you see a stock trade huge volumes with a declining price, you're seeing people dumping the stock like the colonists dumped tea during the Boston Tea Party. If you think the market is right, you too may want to get out of that stock, or you may decide to hold on if you think the market is overreacting. In any case, if you sell when the stock is being dumped like this, don't expect to make much of a profit.

Hi

This figure is the highest price at which the stock traded that day.

Lo

The lowest trading price for the stock that day. The range between the high and low numbers may give you a sense of the volatility of the stock price. If the range is great, it indicates that a lot of conflicting opinions are out there about what the stock is worth. You might be able to take advantage of this volatility over the short term, if you can buy at a low point and sell quickly at a higher point. Of course, this requires that you accurately forecast the future and that you make the proper decisions at the proper times. Almost no one, with the exception of certified psychics, can do this.

Close

This number represents the closing price of the stock for the day. The close is the number that is tracked over time, so when you see stock charts that map a stock's price, you'll usually see points that represent the historical closing prices of the stock. Some charts, as you'll soon see, also keep track of the high and low prices. The closing price for one day generally becomes the opening price of the stock for the next day, unless a

BIG BUCKS

The New York Stock Exchange currently lists the stocks of over 3,000 companies, many of which are the largest and most powerful corporations in the world. There are over **280 billion shares** of stock listed, of which hundreds of millions trade daily. The total market value of all that stock exceeds $16 trillion!

stock is in great demand or is being dumped. In these cases, the price may gap up or gap down to higher or lower prices than the previous day's close.

Net Chg

The net change value compares the closing price for the day with the closing price of the previous trading session. The table for Zza shows that the current closing price for the stock is two points less than the closing price of the previous day. This number fluctuates continually over time, as stock prices go up and down as a matter of course. Your concern is the trend that the stock's price seems to be following. If you see negative numbers in this column day after day for a long time, you're watching a stock that is probably out of favor with the market.

Stock Charts

Now that you know how to interpret a stock table, you're ready to look over a chart of a stock's historical performance. Most charts contain similar information: typically the closing price of a stock each day for a specified period of time and the daily trading volume for that same period. Some charts also display the high and low prices for each trading day. In this case, the price range for the day is indicated as a vertical bar with the top point being the high, the low point being the low, and a notch indicating the closing price for the day. This type of charting is available for free from Bigcharts.com.

From the stock table on page 69, you know that Zza stock recently hit a 52-week high of $143. If you bought Zza stock back in July, when the price tumbled a bit, you'd have made a pretty hefty profit by now. This doesn't mean that the stock is now overpriced or that you missed your opportunity to make money on Zza stock. With a relatively low PE of 23, a history of good earnings and growth, and a sound upward trend in the stock price, Zza may still be quite a nice investment, even at $143 per share.

One mistake novice investors often make is to consider a stock too expensive if the price is over a certain dollar amount. Nothing could be further from the truth. A stock can have a high price per share and still be inexpensive relative to the value of the company and the expected growth of its business. Don't avoid a stock just because it has recently hit an all-time high. The price may indicate that the stock is well on its way to even greater highs.

A stock chart is your best tool for spotting both trends and stock price anomalies. For example, you might be able to glean from Zza's chart that something triggered quite a sell-off in the first couple of weeks in July. If you check the news, you'll find that a rumor was making the rounds on the floor of the NYSE that Zza didn't expect to be able to keep growing at a rate of 75 percent per year forever, because eventually the pizza market would be saturated with Zza stores on every street corner and growth would have to slow down. All the analysts on Wall Street suddenly panicked at the prospect that Zza's amazing growth might someday stop, so they all recommended that their customers sell some of their stock in Zza, just in case. You can see the tremendous rise in volume in the middle of July as the share price dropped in lockstep.

Usually such a combination of high volume with rapid price depreciation spells trouble, but the savvy investor would realize that the market was reacting to nothing but a rumor, and typically rumors have little or no real substance. Judging from its past performance and recent growth, investors had no reason to believe that Zza was heading for troubled times. The panic settled down within days, and Zza stock went right back up. And then a few weeks later, at the beginning of September, Zza once again announced record-breaking earnings, which caused the meteoric rise to $143.

A stock chart is a good source of information on the historical performance of a stock not only because it very clearly shows you price trends over time, but also because you can see the market's reaction to news and rumors that may affect the stock. While knowing the past is not a guarantee that you'll successfully anticipate the future, it can help you forecast how the stock might perform, given a similar set of circumstances. For example, you've seen that a rumor with no basis can have quite a detrimental effect on a stock's price in the short term. If you are confident in your analysis of a company's financial strength and future growth prospects, you may be able to turn this type of situation to your advantage. If you had bought another hundred shares of Zza at $108 on July 13, you'd have made a nice addition to your portfolio.

What's a Share Really Worth?

The value of a company is a measure of what the company is worth in the marketplace as a salable asset. The PE ratio is the most common method used to value a company, largely because it attempts to provide a measurement of the company's worth based on the company's earnings. One popular method of using the PE ratio to determine whether a company's stock is fairly valued is to compare the PE ratio to the growth rate of the company. This method is advocated by Peter Lynch, the great mutual fund manager who steered the Fidelity Magellan fund to stratospheric heights during the 1980s. The idea behind this approach is that for growing companies the PE ratio should be roughly equivalent to the earnings growth of that company. So, for a company that is growing at 75 percent per year, a PE ratio of 75 is not out of line.

Price-to-Sales Ratio

Although the PE ratio is the most widely used method to value a company's shares, it is by no means the only method. Another measure is the price-to-sales ratio (or PSR), which is based not on earnings but on revenues generated by the company. This ratio is calculated by dividing the company's market capitalization by the previous year's total revenues, which you can find on the balance sheet. The market capitalization is defined as the current value of the company, according to the market. This value is determined by multiplying the total number of shares outstanding by the current price per share. For Nellie's Nummy Nuggets, whose recent stock price was $10 per share, the market capitalization would be $70 million (7,000,000 shares outstanding × $10 per share = $70,000,000). To determine the PSR for Nellie's, you'd divide $70 million by $17,500,000 (the revenue amount reported on the company's balance sheet) and arrive at 4. This means that the company is assumed to be worth four times the amount of revenue it is able to generate during the course of a year.

Why would you want to consider the company's revenues rather than earnings as the basis of its valuation? Because sometimes companies go through periods in which no earnings are generated, for one reason or another, but sales are still doing well. Does it seem a little crazy to buy shares of a company with no earnings? Sometimes a company may not yet be able to generate earnings but is nonetheless an attractive investment.

Suppose a new company comes on the scene in a blazingly hot new market. This company may have trouble generating earnings because it is spending lots of money on marketing, research and development, and other business building techniques. Yet its sales may be quite healthy because its market is hot and because the company is ultimately expected to be the dominant player in that market over the next decade. A reasonable way to value such a company is to consider its PSR. It wouldn't even be possible to figure its PE ratio because there wouldn't be any earnings to divide into the price.

Price-to-Book Ratio

Another common method of valuation is to calculate the company's price-to-book ratio. The book value of a company is what you might consider its intrinsic value. This figure represents the actual liquidation value of all the company's assets. Should the company be required to stop doing business immediately and sell itself off in pieces, the book value is the dollar amount that reasonably could be expected to be generated by the sale.

The price-to-book ratio, then, is a good measure of how much the market values the company over and above the intrinsic value of its assets. This ratio is calculated by dividing the current share price by the book value per share. Assuming, for example, that Zza had a book value of $20 per share, its price-to-book ratio at the recent high of $143 would be 7.15 ($143 ÷ $20 = 7.15). This tells you that the market assumes Zza is a good enough company to be able to trade at seven times its book value. Like the PE ratio and the PSR, the price-to-book ratio is a useful tool, but it cannot be considered without taking into account all the other factors that affect the company's future prospects.

The price-to-book ratio may seem at first glance to be the most accurate indicator of a company's worth, because it is based on the company's actual

STOCK TECH

These are some of the major **technological advances** that have affected the stock markets.

1966—First radio pagers in use

1966—First electronic ticker display boards

1976—Designated Order Turnaround (DOT) System devised

book value. However, it is not as widely used as the PE ratio or PSR because the nature of businesses has changed quite a bit over the past few decades. Consider the value of an automobile manufacturer, for example, in contrast to a software manufacturer.

The automobile manufacturer's book value will tell a great deal more about that company than the book value of the software manufacturer, because the automaker's book value includes equipment, plant, materials, and a host of other assets that have real market value apart from what the company produces. The software maker, on the other hand, may rent office space, hire contractors to do programming, and pay another company to manufacture diskettes or CD-ROMs for distribution. The book value of such a company is likely to be low because the value of the company is comprised of intangible assets (like software), which only have value as long as someone wants to use them. The steel used to manufacture automobiles can be used for any number of other things, but a software program is only useful as long as people think it has value. If a competitor comes along with a product that is better, the software company may find itself without any customers and, therefore, with just about no book value.

Taken together, these three measures of a company's value will give you a good indication of how much you should be willing to pay for a stock. Because each measurement considers different aspects of a company's business, you can't just look at one measure or another as the sole indicator of that company's worth.

You need to consider a good deal of other information before deciding that a particular company's PE ratio or PSR is too high or too low. And in some cases, as you've seen, the price-to-book ratio may not be a useful indicator at all. As you continue to invest, you'll learn how to spot situations in which a company is undervalued or overvalued by using the appropriate indicators for that particular situation. Until you're comfortable enough with this kind of analysis, you should try to look at all the indicators you can and the stock tables and historical charts to boot. With time, you'll develop a feel for what looks good about a company and what doesn't.

Yields and Dividends

In general, you can invest in two different types of stocks depending on your goals: growth stocks or income stocks. Growth stocks pay little or no dividends to their

investors, but they promise earnings growth, which will cause the stock's price to appreciate in value over time. They tend to be more volatile or risky than income stocks, which pay regular dividends but which may not appreciate in value as much as growth stocks. Stocks purchased for income tend to be those of larger, more established companies that can afford to share their profits directly with shareholders. The primary difference is the predictability of the income you can expect to earn in a company's stock.

When you invest for growth, you are making the assumption that the company will expand over time into an even more profitable and successful organization. When companies grow and thrive, investors profit because the value of ownership in that company increases. However, the risk inherent in this type of investment is that the company may not succeed in its attempt to become stronger and more profitable. If the company flounders, the value of your investment is likely to decrease, and you'll either try to hold on to the stock in hopes that the company will turn itself around, or you'll be forced to sell your stock at a loss. Investing for growth can take a great deal of stamina and intestinal fortitude because many companies do not, in fact, succeed over the long term. Statistics indicate that only one in five new businesses manage to survive over the first couple of years of their existence, and even fewer survive longer than that. If you become one of the unfortunate people who invests in a company that goes bankrupt, the value of your investment will turn to nothing.

Investors who are interested in making decent returns from their investments without having to absorb as much risk are more likely to invest in income stocks because of the stability of the companies behind them. While it is possible for those stocks to decrease in value like any others, the financial strength of these companies makes this scenario much less likely than for smaller, growing companies. Even if you consider companies like IBM, the shares of which decreased significantly in price between 1987 and 1993, you can still see how large company stocks offer more stability than smaller company

STOCK TECH

These are some of the major **technological advances** that have affected the stock markets.

1978—Intermarket Trading System (ITS) instituted

1983—First Electronic Display Book in use

1994—Internet trading launched

stocks. IBM's shares reached a low of about $25 in 1996 but have since rebounded to their current (as of this writing) level of $120 per share. And although IBM did indeed cut the amount of its dividend during the first part of the 1990s, the company kept paying dividends throughout.

Of course, if you bought shares of IBM at the high price of $174 in 1987, you'd disagree vehemently with the statement that large companies tend to be more stable and solid investments, and you'd be right to feel upset. But this is an extreme example, and the point is that even though IBM's value decreased significantly during this period, the company managed to stay alive and turn itself around despite losing billions of dollars during its toughest times. IBM came back to life, in large part because the company had enough cash and resource reserves to weather the storm for a number of years. Smaller companies would have long since disappeared into oblivion.

Dividend Yield

By investing for income or dividends, you are investing in more established companies that would be more likely to survive even during difficult economic times. And when good times roll around, your investment could, just like any other, increase in value just as well as a smaller growth stock. If you bought shares of IBM stock at its low in 1993, your stock's value would have quadrupled by 1999. While this kind of growth is unpredictable (for instance, IBM's dividends in the year 2000 are a fraction of what they were in 1997), you can generally count on reliable dividends from companies that pay them and determine the percentage of yield that your investment will earn for you, just as if you were to invest your money in a bank account.

The dividend yield of a stock is calculated by dividing the annual dividend by the price you paid per share of stock. So, if you purchased IBM stock at $100, and your annual dividend is $5 per share, your dividend yield on this investment would be 5 percent ($5 ÷ $100 = .05 × 100 = 5%).

One reason for calculating the dividend yield is to make comparisons between different types of investments. While the investor who seeks to profit from growth has little basis for comparison between the growth stock and other investments because of the unpredictability of that growth, the income-minded investor can compare the div-

idend yield to yields offered by such investments as bonds, bond funds, bank accounts, money markets, and the like. If you purchase a stock that offers you a dividend yield of 5 percent, are you better off there than in a money market fund paying 5 percent, or in a bond paying 4 percent? With stocks, you always have the advantage of moving your investment dollars elsewhere at any time and with the possibility of capital appreciation. Over time, you could be looking at a very nice investment. Money market funds and bonds may give similar returns to stocks, but they require a longer-term commitment of your funds in order to realize those returns.

However, stocks also have the potential downside of capital losses, so you have to weigh the potential benefits against your willingness to accept different levels of risk. While the money market fund only pays 5 percent, you are practically guaranteed not to lose the principal value of your investment (the money you invested in the first place). And the bond offers the comfort that if the company goes out of business, you, as a bondholder, are more likely to receive something back from the liquidation of the company's assets than a stockholder. So while investing in income-producing stocks may be a less risky way of profiting from the growth of companies than investing strictly for growth, nothing guarantees that you won't lose money in the market.

TRIPLE-WITCHING DAYS

While the movement of the stock market in general is unpredictable, certain events cause similar reactions in the market each and every time they occur.

One of these is the triple-witching day, which occurs quarterly. On every third Friday of March, June, September, and December, the following all expire simultaneously: stock options, stock index options, and stock index futures. This occurrence causes a lot of volatility, as market traders scramble to cover positions in financial instruments based on stocks. A lot of volatility resides in the underlying stocks themselves, leading to wide price swings throughout the day.

If you're accustomed to watching your stocks' prices change throughout the day, hold on to your hat on triple-witching day—you're likely to see some serious rollercoaster pricing action.

GET *those* feet wet, or *where to* BEGIN

CHAPTER FOUR

Now that you know the history of the stock market and the concepts and activities that make it **hum** like a well-oiled engine at the Indy 500, it's time to call a **broker** or two, open some accounts, and start saving. Your broker is your investing partner. **Follow him or her wisely.**

Brokers are like your investing partners. You should feel that you can count on them to follow through on the orders you place, and you should be confident that they'll lead you to profitable investments that you might not have found on your own. You need to find brokers who are reputable and honest and who suit your investment style and respect your investment decisions.

You may have heard horror stories that make you want to lump stockbrokers into the same category as shady, used-car salesmen and discoverers of the fountain of youth. The industry does have its fair share of snake oil salesmen who will try to sell you

shares in the Brooklyn Bridge, if you let them. But if you're smart and savvy enough, you'll be able to recognize these shysters when they sneak up on you.

How do you know who is the right partner for your investing activities? Sometimes you have to follow your instincts. If you get a slightly queasy feeling in your stomach, which tells you something's not quite right, go with it and walk right out of the broker's office—after extracting your hand from that much-too-firm-and-aggressive handshake.

If you're a self-starter and would rather do your own research and pick your own stocks, you may not want to deal with a broker at all. Numerous discount and deep-discount brokerage services allow you to trade without a particular broker acting as your agent. And, in this Internet-enabled day and age, plenty of services allow you to trade online right from your home computer, so you don't even have to talk to anyone about the stocks you're buying and selling.

How a Broker Makes Money

The fee structure in some segments of the brokerage industry is set up to reward brokers not for being successful in managing your money, but for moving your money around as much as possible. These brokers are paid by transaction, not by their success in managing their clients' accounts. In other words, every time you buy shares or sell shares, your broker makes something just for handling the order. While this practice is not necessarily wrong per se, sometimes the fees can be quite substantial for the amount of work the broker does to fill an order. Before you get involved with any broker, find out how she makes her money.

Many full-service brokers are compensated based on the amount of assets under management. So, as your assets grow, so do your broker's. Your broker's advantage, therefore, lies in making you money. Take care to ensure that you're getting what you want from your broker, not what the broker wants. When a broker moves your money into and out of stocks relatively frequently, without paying much attention to whether or not these moves are actually profitable to you, the investor, he may be churning. Brokers can still make a lot of money even if they don't churn your account, as long as you keep buying and/or selling shares of stock. So when a broker calls you daily to "let you in on a hot stock deal," be careful and make sure the company is really a good invest-

WHO'S LOOKING OUT FOR YOU?

While you may sometimes feel very much alone out there in the investment jungle, you can feel heartened to know that some people and organizations are on your side. The SEC, for example, is a watchdog organization that keeps tabs on activities in the marketplace, keeping abuses to a minimum. The National Association of Individual Investors (NAII) is another association that provides information to individual investors in the larger marketplace. The NAII also provides educational services to assist investors in becoming knowledgeable participants in the free-market system. If you're having trouble understanding how some things work or you need help with what you think may be a genuine scam, you should get in touch with the NAII. You can contact the NAII on the Internet at <www.naiix.org>.

ment before you toss your hard-earned cash into it. Whether that deal earns you any money or causes you to lose your shirt, your broker makes money simply by virtue of your purchase of the stock.

Why You Need a Broker

Despite the fact that sometimes the relationship between a broker and an investor can become a tense and uncomfortable affair—imagine how you'd feel about your broker if you bought on his latest recommendation and lost a bunch of money—nonetheless, you do need someone to act as an intermediary between yourself and the larger market. You can't go down to the local stock exchange, walk up to a bulletproof Plexiglas® window, plop down a pile of dollars, and order shares of ZYX stock. The exchanges are private organizations, which require membership to directly participate in their activities—and the price of a seat on an exchange can be prohibitive for all but the most well-heeled investors. To buy or sell stocks that are traded on an exchange, you need an agent with an exchange membership to place those transactions for you. Most individual brokers don't have seats themselves, but they work for member firms that do have seats on the various exchanges. This membership allows them to act as intermediaries between you, the individual investor, and the marketplace.

The securities industry is highly regulated and carefully watched over. Member firms must not only have exchange membership, but also the government must license them to provide investment services. Individuals who work as brokers in licensed member firms pass a series of qualifying examinations that test their knowl-

edge of the industry, so they can offer advice and information that is accurate and sensible. Even discount and deep-discount brokerage firms are required to be licensed to work in the securities industry. And if you use the newer online investment services over the Internet, or services like America Online or CompuServe, you'll still be dealing, albeit indirectly, with licensed brokers who are able to act as agents for your transactions.

The over-the-counter market, or Nasdaq, operates in an arena in which there is no exchange to speak of, although here, too, plenty of rules and regulations affect trading. The Nasdaq brokers typically act as "market makers" who are responsible for buying and selling stocks to the public. If your broker is a market maker for stock A, but you want to buy stock B, your broker has to contact the market maker for stock B and borrow shares from that company before being able to sell them to you.

As you can see, buying stocks is not like going to the local supermarket for a box of cereal and a gallon of milk. The stock market and the securities industries are very complex interrelationships of companies doing business on many levels. You'll always have to deal with some sort of middleman when you're buying or selling stocks, so you should work to overcome any distaste you may have for this necessity and save your energy to decide which brokers to use.

The kind of brokerage you end up with will depend ultimately on what you require. Basically, three types of brokers offer varying degrees of service: full-service, discount, and deep-discount. Other market players exist, but they generally don't offer retail services to individual investors, or if they do, their services are part of the package provided by one of these three categories of firms. For example, your discount broker might be a market maker in a number of stocks, and your full-service broker probably has a number of traders on the floors of various exchanges. You won't directly come across these people in your day-to-day investing activities, so for the purpose of considering brokers as investment agents that can buy or sell shares for your account, you don't need to worry about them.

Full-Service Brokers

A full-service broker is the most expensive broker you'll encounter as you journey into the stock market. Whether or not the services provided are worth the extra money is a question only you can answer for yourself. It's a bit like the full-service pump at the gas station. You don't want to get out of your car in the cold to deal with the pump and get gas fumes in your head and on your hands, but is full service worth the extra quarter per gallon? For some people it is. For others, it seems like an absurd waste of money. Your attitude really depends on what you want out of the situation. If you're dressed to the nines for a night out and don't want to smell like an oil tanker when you get to the theater, then maybe full service is the way to go. But if you won't have any money left for a glass of wine at intermission, maybe you should pump the darned gas yourself.

When you use a full-service broker, you're paying for the dedicated activity of an investment professional who can keep an eye on your investments day after day, make recommendations on what stocks to buy or sell, research and investigate new opportunities, and try to balance your portfolio to match your individual investment goals as much as possible. This really is the dirty work of investing, the details that lots of people simply would rather not do at all. You can even set up a discretionary trading account, giving your broker the power to make trading decisions for certain periods of time or in certain circumstances. Investing wisely does take a certain amount of time, so that you can track your investments and make decisions about your portfolio. If you have neither the time nor the inclination to do this kind of work, a full-service broker may be just what you need.

VOLUMINOUS TRADING ACTIVITIES

Investors have become accustomed to hearing about stock market trading volume in the hundreds of millions of shares per day, so it's hard to imagine a time when daily trading volume wasn't always so high. In fact, the first time daily trading volume exceeded 100 million shares was only as recently as August 18, 1982. The lowest trading volume of any active trading day on the NYSE occurred on March 16, 1830, when only 31 shares changed hands.

These brokerage firms offer many other services in addition to the retail services for individual investors, and these services all play a part in the cost structure the firm charges you for investing. Most full-service firms not only have a retail division to offer retail services, they also have a research division and an investment banking division. You'll spend most of your time interacting with the retail division when you deal with a full-service firm. This is also the company's sales division, and this is

where the brokers work. The reason for this division's existence is to sell stocks to investors. The more stock they sell, the more commissions they make.

The research division of a brokerage is made up of armies of analysts who study stocks day after day and write reports either recommending or not recommending those stocks. These reports, or parts of them, are occasionally published in the financial press. You'll often see analysts' recommendations (typically ex cathedra pronouncements such as, "Buy!" "Sell!" or "Hold!") or earnings expectations published in *The Wall Street Journal, Investor's Business Daily,* or more specialized newsletters such as *Zacks Investment Research.* These recommendations and earnings forecasts come from the desks of the analysts at larger brokerage firms, which have the resources to subsidize entire research divisions dedicated to analyzing stocks.

Whether or not the analysts turn out to be right is something that time determines. If you use a full-service brokerage firm for your investing activities, you'll very likely have access to more detailed research reports than are published in the widely distributed press. This information is part of the service you pay for at a full-service brokerage, and it may be worth its weight in gold. Then again, it may not. Today, thanks to the electronic revolution with the Internet at its lead, individual investors have easy access to significant resources that were never readily available before.

The investment banking division of a full-service brokerage firm is the division that deals directly with companies that are issuing shares of stock to the public. When a company decides to go public and begin selling shares to investors, the investment banking division of a brokerage firm steps in to underwrite that stock offering. This process is complex and time consuming, but it is the primary way that big brokerage firms make their money. Even if the firm has lots of investors paying big fees for buying and selling stocks, the firm as a whole makes a great deal more money from investment banking operations than from retail sales.

Each company that issues stock in an initial public offering (IPO) has to pay a percentage of the earnings from that IPO to the brokerage firm as payment for its services. The money generated by IPOs is often in the multimillions of dollars, and the percentages earned by investment bankers are a nice chunk of the pie. If the company underwrites a number of IPOs or additional stock offerings during the course of a year, that firm is likely to be making a pot of money in the process.

A Conflict of Interest?

Should you take the research and advice of a full-service broker at face value? With one side of its business underwriting public offerings of stock and the other side trying to sell as much of this stock as possible, you may be right in feeling a little squeamish about buying stocks just because your broker says you should. And you may want to take the output of the research department with a grain of salt as well, because any research provided about a stock that this brokerage has underwritten may have more than a slight bias to it.

When your broker calls you in the middle of the night bubbling over about an exciting new offering, make sure you get your hands on some concrete numbers (balance sheet, income statement, and the like) before you take the plunge. If your broker's firm also happens to be the underwriter for this offering, the investment banking division is probably applying some pressure to sell the stock. And the sale will generate even more money for the brokerage firm from the commissions you'll pay for the purchase. However, to say that every single full-service broker out there is just pushing stocks that the investment banking group has decided to underwrite, regardless of their underlying value, would be an unfair generalization.

Many pressures bear upon brokers, and one of them is certainly the sales quotas they've got to meet on a monthly or quarterly basis. On the other hand, just because a broker is trying to sell you a stock for which the firm has acted as the investment banker doesn't mean that stock is necessarily a bad investment. You may have a golden opportunity to get in on the ground floor of something that turns out to be the investment of a lifetime. But it's ultimately up to you to do follow-up research to make sure the numbers look good.

With a full-service broker, doing this research should be no more difficult than simply asking your broker to send you copies of the company's financials. If you sense any reluctance when you request this information, consider it a red flag and avoid the stock, no matter how certain the broker seems to be about its being a sure thing. It will always be a sure thing for your broker when you buy more stock. On the other hand, although brokers aren't affected directly by the risks you take in the market, if they recommend a string of losing stocks, they're likely to lose you as a good customer.

Taking a look at a full-service broker's investment history, before you sign up for services, is important. If you can find someone you are comfortable with and feel you can trust, try to talk to other people who have worked with this individual before. If the broker is up to snuff, she should have no problem providing you with some references from happy customers. Make sure to ask a lot of questions, and if you don't like any of the answers move on. (See page 97 for a list of some of the questions you may want to ask brokers and references.) It's your money, and you're paying dearly for what should be a very valuable and profitable service. But you cannot afford to pay those high, full-service brokerage fees to someone who isn't willing to spend time working with you to manage your portfolio and provide you with the best possible returns. You can lose enough money on your own in the market—why should you add insult to injury paying high commissions for the privilege of having someone else lose it for you?

Discount Brokers

A relatively new category of brokerage service evolved with the advent of speedy electronic communications and an important event that occurred in 1975. That year, the Securities and Exchange Commission (SEC) changed the pricing structure that had long determined commissions for buying and selling stocks. Prior to 1975, commissions were based on a fixed system that applied across the entire brokerage industry. You'd choose a broker on the basis of recommendations or other services offered, but not typically on commission rates, because these generally were the same throughout the industry. In 1975, the SEC changed the rules; they banned fixed minimum commission rates and declared that brokerage firms could charge whatever they considered appropriate. The SEC implemented rules and guidelines to keep customers from being gouged by unscrupulous brokers, but the upshot is that the new regulations opened the door to a new type of brokerage firm: the discount brokerage.

Discount brokerage firms began offering customers an alternative to the expensive commissions charged by full-service firms. Technological improvements also contributed to the growth of the discount brokerage industry, because not as many people needed to be involved with the process of buying and selling stocks. Computers could transmit orders directly to the trading floor or even execute specified transactions directly with the markets. This improvement in efficiency, along with the change in the pricing structure of conducting stock transactions, led to a price war that has yet

Why Can't You Buy Stocks Directly?

The stock exchanges are private organizations that require expensive memberships and government approval to join. The Nasdaq and over-the-counter markets are operated by market makers and broker/dealers who buy and sell shares to the market through other brokers who sell to retail investors.

Market makers or broker/dealers need organizations with a great deal of capital to be able to buy and sell very large blocks of stock. The entire market system is a complicated and changing environment, in which transactions occur 24 hours a day, 7 days a week—but this doesn't happen in a central location and the whole mechanism isn't managed by any single group.

Because of the complexity of the marketplace and the potential that exists for abuse, it is highly regulated by the government. While wealthy investors often purchase seats on an exchange in order to buy and sell stocks for their own accounts, most individual investors aren't able to meet the financial requirements and must therefore trade stocks by using the services of an agent or broker.

The rules and structures of the market weren't set up to discriminate against the small investor, however, but to provide a relatively efficient method of conducting stock transactions by the greatest number of people possible. If millions of investors had direct access to the markets, the result could be chaos. The brokerage system is actually a positive and effective way to manage a system this big and elaborate. Things change, however, and innumerable companies now allow you to purchase stocks directly, bypassing the brokers. These are known as "no-load stocks."

to see its end. Discount brokerage firms popped up in all parts of the country, each one offering better pricing than the other. In fact, as these firms grew and multiplied, they began to compete on the basis of a more old-fashioned concept—service. It does seem paradoxical that discount brokerage firms, companies that came into being on the basis of cheaper pricing for stock orders, would wind up competing on the same turf as their full-service brethren, but prices can only go so low.

If you're considering two or three potential discounters, all of which offer the same basic pricing, the services provided will be the basis of your decision. If one discount broker offers you research reports at no extra charge, then you might consider that firm a better place to park your money.

How do discount brokerage firms differ from full-service brokers? Most discount firms are strictly retail-oriented operations. They don't have investment banking or research divisions like full-service firms. The discount brokerage firm typically offers little or no investment guidance but simply places orders for individual investors as an agent. The fact that these firms don't tend to offer advice and don't have other divisions means that they can streamline their operations to keep costs down, and then they can pass these lower costs to you, the investor. However, because many discount brokerage firms have begun to compete on the basis of service rather than simply price, you're likely to come across discount brokerage firms that provide news and research services to their customers. Providing more service means increased cost to you, but you're still likely to pay quite a bit less for the services of discount brokers than those of full-service brokers.

The biggest difference between full-service and discount brokers revolves around getting investment advice and guidance. Full-service firms tend to have a hold on that one area because the commissions you pay them assume that they're providing you with some sort of financial counseling as well as placing your trades for you. Usually your account representative at a full-service brokerage firm has a good handle on your financial situation, in contrast to representatives at discount firms. In fact, the full-service firms tend to call their representatives investment advisors rather than account executives. With a full-service firm, you should expect your advisor to become a close financial partner who can help you make investment decisions. With a discount firm, you're generally on your own unless you get research reports and/or news to help you determine your investments.

Deep-Discount Brokers

Because the competition among discount brokers heated up as more of them entered the fray and began to add more services to distinguish themselves from their competitors, a third category of brokerage firm evolved. Deep-discounters, the lowest echelon of brokerages, offer the lowest possible prices and just about nothing extra in the way of services. These firms let you do your own research with your own tools and your own decision making with your own mind. And they can give you up to a 90 percent discount on full-service rates.

If you're the kind of person who likes to control your own financial destiny, a deep-discount firm might be your best choice. Most of them will simply take your orders and place them for you, and possibly offer a quotation service where you'll be able to get the latest stock quotes. Apart from that, they'll usually offer nothing else but very, very low commissions.

Picking the Right Broker

When you're choosing a broker, you've got to determine what kind of service is important to you and how much you're willing to pay for it. The pricing differences among the three primary types of brokerages are quite significant, so you really have to be sure the money you're spending on commissions is paid back to you in profitable investments. One advantage of using a full-service broker, for example, is that you might have the option of buying stock at its opening price during the IPO of an interesting new company. Generally, with discount or deep-discount brokers, you won't have the opportunity to buy stock at its opening price during an IPO because those shares are initially only available from the underwriter of that IPO. In some cases, getting in early on the IPO of a hot new stock could make a huge difference in the amount of profit you can expect from an investment.

Another advantage of full-service brokerage is that you'll most likely have a competent and experienced advisor working for you and watching over your portfolio all the time. If you aren't interested in spending the time it takes to research stocks and make your own investment decisions, the extra cost for full-service brokerage might be money well spent.

But if you are more interested in saving money on transaction costs and don't mind doing your own homework to find out about stocks, a discount or deep-discount broker might be a better choice. Investment research is widely available from a number of places, so you don't have to rely on the efforts of your full-service broker to provide you with this information. From financial publications like *The Wall Street Journal, Investor's Business Daily, Forbes, Fortune,* and many others, to private newsletters and services like *Zacks Investment Research* and *The Value Line Investment Survey,* you have a plethora of sources from which to get your investment information. And, if you are a "wired investor" and are familiar with services like America Online, CompuServe, or that mother of all electronic universes, the Internet, you already have access right at your fingertips to some of the best possible investment research and information you are likely to encounter anywhere.

The only considerations about using discount or deep-discount services are how much you'll actually pay per transaction and whether you have the time and interest to dig around for your own investment information. If you are willing to spend a little time doing the necessary research, you can be the best investment advisor you'll ever meet for your own needs.

Another exciting development is that these days, you can use online services for far more than simply finding information about investments. Most brokerage firms, from the top-tier, full-service outfits to the ultra-cheapest, deep-deep-discount, no-frills-even-if-you-want-'em companies, offer online transaction services so you can place your trades directly. Depending on the type of company you use, you may also have online access to that company's research department, a stock quotation service, and more. When seeking out a firm, make sure the services offered are what you need.

If you aren't online, don't want to do your own research, or would rather just let someone else make your financial decisions for you, then by all means try to find a good full-service broker with a

STOCK TECH

These are some of the major **technological advances** that have affected the stock markets.

1994 to 1996— Integrated Technology Network developed

1995—First IPO launched over the Internet

1996—Wireless Data System introduced

solid track record—someone you feel you can trust. If you're wired, enjoy the process of finding things out for yourself, and would rather die than let someone else tell you where to put your money, a discount or deep-discount firm is probably for you.

Some Questions to Ask a Potential Broker

- Get references about the company as well as about the individual broker you're working with. For larger, well-known firms such as Merrill Lynch, you may not need a reference for the company itself, but make sure to get references for the individual broker. All kinds of brokers are out there, even within the same company, so make sure you are at ease with the one you're dealing with.

- Ask when you can meet face-to-face. Set up an appointment in the broker's office or somewhere else where you can discuss your investing goals and ask some questions about the broker's investing style. Remember that this person is going to be managing your money. Are they someone you feel you can trust?

- Ask if the broker would discuss your investments with other professionals with whom you may have arrangements, such as your attorney or your accountant. If the broker is unwilling to face such scrutiny, move on to another one.

- When you talk to the broker's references, ask them if they've been pleased with the service. If not, find out what they don't like. Everyone will have different reactions to different people and different levels of service. Make sure you make your judgments on the basis of things that are important to you.

- See how the broker responds to your investment goals. If, for example, you are primarily interested in purchasing income stocks for dividends and you want to avoid risk as much as possible, but the broker keeps trying to talk you into buying high-flying, risky stocks that are "sure to make you rich," make sure you walk out the door. Avoid high-pressure salespersons if they make you nervous or uneasy or if they don't listen to what you are saying.

- Does the broker respond promptly to your phone calls? If you're paying fees for service, you should expect to receive service, particularly if you're dealing with an expensive, full-service firm.

- Be sure to get very specific numbers when you ask to see the company's commission schedule. You don't want to get any unpleasant commission surprises when you buy a stock. Most firms have a graded commission arrangement, whereby trading prices depend on a number of factors, such as the number of shares traded and the cost per share. You'll often pay a higher commission on shares with a higher price. Some companies, usually the deep-discounters, offer fixed-rate fees for any size transaction. Try to find a firm that offers the best prices for the types of transactions you are most likely to do.

- Is the broker too busy to keep a close watch on your account? Imagine that you open an account with a full-service firm only to discover later that your broker has too many clients to give you the attention you deserve. You can end up paying expensive commissions for little service.

- If you're considering a discount or deep-discount firm, try to find out from other customers whether the firm has been responsive and placed their trades efficiently. Sometimes smaller firms don't have the resources to place buy or sell orders for all their customers quickly. If you are in a hurry to unload a particular stock because you see it dropping rapidly through the floor, you won't be happy if your cheap-discount firm can't get the order to the NYSE floor before tomorrow morning.

- Find out if you'll get information in a timely manner when promising opportunities become available. This consideration is probably most relevant to full-service brokers because discounters and deep-discounters aren't going to be watching your portfolio for you. But if your broker knows about a potentially great investment and doesn't bother to get in touch with you quickly enough so you can take advantage of it, the price you're paying for the service just isn't worth it.

Can You Trust Your Broker?

This is a question only you will be able to answer, but here are some tips that can help you make this determination.

Are you using the services of a full-service broker? If so, then your broker probably has much more direct access to your account than if you were to use a discount or deep-discount broker. What is your full-service broker's track record with regard to the investments that have been made for you? Is the broker always buying shares of stock for which the brokerage firm is also acting as the underwriter? If so, are you pleased with the results of the investments? Remember that even though you've agreed to allow your broker to manage your investments for you, you are still ultimately responsible for your money, and you need to keep a close watch on where it goes.

If you're using the services of a deep-discount broker, you're usually on your own as far as your investment decisions go, but if you are using a discount broker, you may need to find out if the brokerage firm is a market maker or dealer for any particular stocks, which means that they have a vested interest in selling as much of that stock as possible.

Before you purchase any stock on the recommendation of your broker, make sure you've done your research about the investment and feel comfortable with it. If you buy a stock because you were pressured into it by a fast-talking salesperson, you'll have no one to blame but yourself if the stock turns out to be a loser.

- Ask about the interest rate the firm charges for margin accounts. Buying on margin means that you're borrowing money from the brokerage firm to purchase stocks. But you're going to pay interest on these loans, so if you plan to buy on margin, try to find a firm with the best possible rates.

- Find out if the firm offers at least a basic quotation service. Even deep-discount firms often have toll-free numbers that you can call to place trades and get stock quotes. If you like to keep up with your investments but don't know at what price your stocks are trading, you won't be able to make decent buy and sell decisions.

Get Online

A great place to find answers to many of these questions is the online world. Most services have chat and discussion areas where you can talk about your goals and investments with thousands of other small investors like yourself. And the Internet has Usenet newsgroups, large bulletin boards dedicated to discussions of all sorts of subjects. You can post a question to one of these discussion areas, and within hours you'll have answers from potentially hundreds of people. So, if you're thinking that OLDE Discount Brokerage is the firm you want to use as your primary brokerage, but you don't have any references and don't know anyone who has used OLDE's service, you can log in to your online service and read the opinions of lots of people who have had experience with OLDE.

In this day and age, the online world really should be thought of as the investor's best friend. So much information and so many people are out there, and you can reap such tremendous benefits from being online, that there's not much excuse for not getting out there. The Internet is one of the most valuable tools you can use to help with your investing activities.

You Need a Financial Checkup

Before you start tossing money into the stock market, hoping to make a killing in the latest and greatest companies, you need to do at least a perfunctory evaluation of your general financial health and well-being. Investing in the market involves risk, so you

should make sure first and foremost that you are financially able to accept and deal with this risk. The greatest risk you face as a stock investor is that you could lose all the money you invest. Such a painfull loss can be offset somewhat if you take a balanced and carefully considered approach to your finances.

Take Care of Debt First

Any money you invest in stocks should be considered risk money, money that is expendable and not necessary to keep you, your family, and your dogs and cats alive. Creditors, while occasionally capable of understanding, and sometimes even human, are not a friendly lot when you start missing your payments on a regular basis. Pay the mortgage, pay the car payment, and by all means get rid of those credit card debts. You will most likely be paying far more in interest on those things than you will make in the market (at least initially), so the idea of paying the minimum amounts due on your credit cards and putting the rest of your money into the market should immediately be banished from the realm of your thoughts. Don't even toy with this option. If you think you've got a line on a stock that is going to make you rich, you may be right— this time. But don't look for any sympathy when that killer penny stock winds up killing your finances and your creditors put a lien on your house because you've got no money left to pay the bills. Pay down debts first, then invest.

Think about Diversification

This means that you distribute your money and investments among a variety of stocks and other types of investments. You may be thinking, "But if I put all my money in Zza stock a couple of years ago, I'd be loaded by now!" You might be right about that. So why didn't you think of that when Zza first went public? Is it, perhaps, because you, like the rest of us, are not able to predict the future? Yes, investment research pays off. Picking stocks of good, solid companies in healthy, stable industries will usually result in profits over time. But success is not guaranteed by any means. Suppose the general economy enters a recession and your one and only company is negatively impacted. Or further suppose that the hot industry that you decided to get in on suddenly grows very cold and everyone pulls their money out. It's a cliché, but it needs to be said anyway: Don't put all your eggs in one basket. Try to build a portfolio of investments in different types of stocks or even buy shares in a bond fund or two. While

taking great risks can, and sometimes does, result in fantastic profits, not losing all your money has more advantages. Know the difference between taking calculated and well-considered risks and simply throwing caution to the wind.

Never, Ever Bet the Ranch

No matter how much money your broker or your friends say you'll make on a stock, don't risk everything on a single stock. You and everyone else can probably recount stories of those unbelievable stocks that you never bought that rose in value by a factor of 500 over a two-year period. If you had bet the ranch on that amazing stock, you could be a multimillionaire living on a sunny beach somewhere in the tropics today. But we all know about plenty of other stocks that have lost 100 percent of their value in a year as well.

If you remember anything at all from this book, let it be that there is no such thing as a sure thing! Keep your financial house clean, and you won't live to regret it.

Initial Investments

The idea that you have to be wealthy to be an investor in the stock market is a misconception. The amount of the initial investment required to open a brokerage account varies greatly among the various classes of brokerage firms, and within those classes among the firms themselves. While some brokerage firms cater to the well-heeled and require you to have at least half a million dollars before they'll even talk to you, plenty of other firms will be pleased to do business with you, even if you only have a small amount of cash on hand. Some firms will let you open an account with only $1,000.

When you open a brokerage account, you'll be asked to fill out a few forms that disclose your financial condition to the brokerage firm. They're not trying to pry into your personal matters. Laws dictate how brokerage firms must act in regard to their customers, and some of these rules require you to have a certain amount of financial stability before you are allowed to open a brokerage account.

Another reason these disclosures are necessary is so that your broker will have an objective idea of exactly how much you can actually afford to lose. Some people will get

Considering Spreads

While advantageous to you to be aware of and to minimize the amount of money you spend on taxes and commissions, another hidden cost is associated with investing in certain markets. This cost is known as the spread between the bid price and the asking price of a stock.

When you purchase a stock, you will always be paying the asking price for that stock. When you attempt to sell that stock later, you will receive the bid price. This difference is based on what dealers are willing to pay for a stock in comparison to what they are willing to sell that same stock for. The difference between these prices is usually fairly small on a per share basis, but when you consider trades consisting of large numbers of shares, you may be paying a substantial additional premium for your investment.

Usually you don't pay much attention to this spread, even if it's provided by your broker, because typically you don't sell immediately after making your investment, but the difference between the bid and ask is another method by which brokers and dealers can profit from their roles as agents in the stock market. However, if you purchase shares of a stock with a very low trading price and low daily trading volume, the spread may be significant as a percentage of the stock's total price.

You'll have to hold on to those shares a bit longer not only to make a profit from the company's increasing value, but also to make up for the spread that's built into the quoted price.

so worked up about a stock that they'll try to invest every dime they own in it. Your financial disclosures will keep your brokers informed about what you can really invest, so that they don't encourage you to spend money you don't have and can't afford to borrow. For example, the disclosure statements are used to determine how much stock you can buy on margin. If you could buy as much as you wanted on margin, and then the stocks you bought slowly swirled their way down the proverbial toilet, you would be in some seriously dire straits. The SEC requires investors to disclose their financial condition in part as a means of protecting investors from themselves.

Generally speaking, full-service brokerage firms have more stringent financial require-ments for initial investments than discount or deep-discount firms, but this isn't a hard and fast rule. Once you've decided on the type of company you want to work with, make a few phone calls to find out exactly what you'll need to have available to open an investment account. In addition to a minimum required to open an account, some firms also may want you to keep a certain amount of money available in their money market or cash account to protect them from losing money if you have investments on margin. When brokers lend you money on margin, their main priority is to make sure that money eventually gets paid back. When you buy stocks on margin, you're not only risking your own money, you're risking your broker's money as well. It's only reasonable to expect that the brokerage firms will do whatever they can to protect themselves.

Tread Carefully . . . and Don't Forget about Those Commissions

A few words of caution now that you've chosen your broker, gotten rid of your debt, and lined up your cash ready to invest. Before you start buying and selling stocks like a pro, you need to keep these points in mind. First of all, be careful out there. Lots of people, who are very slick and savvy, know how to make a buck at someone else's ex-pense. Don't buy stocks without doing your homework. Make sure you really like the company's financials before you throw your money into the ring. This point cannot be overemphasized.

Even if your broker is the most honest and genuinely helpful human being on the planet, plenty of other people are going to try to get their hands on your money. As

SITTING DOWN AT THE EXCHANGE

Since everyone stands and runs and shouts on the floor of the NYSE, why is a membership called a seat? The history of the term comes from the days prior to 1971 when stocks were traded in what was known as a call market. Stock exchange **members** were each assigned a particular seat (literally) at the exchange. When it came time to trade, a caller would call out each stock to be traded one at a time, and the members would then make their buy and sell offers. When they were finished, the next stock would be called.

soon as you start investing, your name will wind up on mailing and telemarketing lists of all sorts, and you'll soon get offers for this or that wonderful investment. If you trust your broker and have a good relationship, ask for an opinion about those stocks. Get online and get feedback from people on the Internet. Check the SEC's Web site for information about the company. Don't buy anything that you don't understand and that you can't find any information about. Many authentic investment opportunities are out there, and you don't want to waste your time on junk.

Don't forget about the commission costs involved with every transaction you make. If you buy a stock and sell it a week later, you may make a profit, but if your commissions are greater than or equal to that profit, where has the profit gone? Commissions are generated on every buy and every sell transaction you make, so factor them in right from the start. You could potentially make lots of money by buying and selling stocks over short periods of time, but the more transactions you generate, the more money you'll be paying in commissions. And they generally aren't a trivial cost. Even if your deep-discount firm only charges you $20 per trade, that's a total of $40 for every buy-sell pairing, about the cost of a nice dinner or a few beers with your friends. If you multiply that $40 by ten different stocks over a month, you're looking at $400 in commissions—and that's with a deep-discount firm. Imagine your costs if you trade like this using a full-service broker.

Finally, don't forget about your greedy Uncle Sam. Whenever you make even the smallest profit on a stock transaction, he'll be there waiting for his cut. Taxes can kill profits as fast as high commissions can, so remember to factor these in, as well. If you make $100 profit on the purchase and sale of a stock, but pay out $40 in commissions

and another $30 in taxes, you aren't going to have very much left for yourself. Don't buy and sell needlessly. Be prudent and sell only when you feel right about it, not because you get nervous or because you want to lock in a small amount of profit. Small profits turn into practically no profits after commissions and taxes have been extracted from your unwilling hands.

SO *what's* a market *index* ANYWAY?

CHAPTER FIVE

*The process of valuing a stock is very **important** for investors. Valuing a stock correctly gives you a better shot at predicting how it will **perform.***

In Chapter Three you learned about various ways to determine the fair value of a stock based on the "fundamentals" (the company's underlying financial situation). The process of valuing a stock is very important for investors, because it helps them know whether or not the price they're paying for a stock is appropriate and whether it is reasonable to expect to profit from their investment. But what if you want to measure the performance of the market as a whole? Is there any way to determine whether or not the performance of your investments is where it should be in relation to that broader market? In fact, rather than just one way to benchmark the performance of the market, numerous measurements are used to determine the value of entire sectors of the mar-

ket, as well as measurements for the market as a whole. These measures are known as market averages or market indexes.

The Thumbnail History of Market Averages

The first average used to measure the performance of the stock market was created by Charles Dow in 1884. Dow, along with his partner Edward Jones, founded Dow Jones & Company in 1882 to provide investors with timely and relevant information about stocks and the markets in which they traded. The most widely known publication of Dow Jones is *The Wall Street Journal,* one of the best sources of business and stock market information in the world.

When Dow created his now famous market average, his goal was to provide investors with a measuring stick with which to determine the overall strength or weakness of the American economy and that of the stock markets themselves. The initial average created by Dow was comprised of the stocks of 11 railroad companies. At the time, the railroads were one of the strongest industries in America, so the average was thought to be a good indicator of the strength of the overall economy. Over the years, Dow added to and substituted stocks in his list, and by 1897 the average included the stocks of 20 railroad companies. Dow Jones & Company also created another index in 1897 that was based on the stock performance of a dozen industrial companies.

These indexes were finely tuned over the years, and today Dow Jones & Company maintains three primary indexes: the Dow Jones Industrial Average, the Dow Jones Transportation Average, and the Dow Jones Utilities Average. The Dow Jones Composite Average is a fourth average that monitors the stocks in all three of the other averages.

What Do the Indexes Mean to You?

The Dow Jones averages are only a few of the dozens of market indexes that are tracked and reported daily in the financial news. They are used to determine the health of the stock market as well as the health of the overall economy. Investment activity tends to be high when the economy is strong and vice versa. The markets and the general economy are very closely related, so the stock market indexes can be used to mea-

sure economic strength or weakness in all sectors of the economy. While you as an investor are primarily interested in the performance of your own investments, the averages and indexes can be used to help you make investment decisions based on general trends in the markets.

As you become more perceptive about investing, you will begin to see patterns in the movements of the stock market indexes, which you can use as guidelines to determine an appropriate course of action for the management of your own investment portfolio. For example, if you are invested in a number of transportation-oriented stocks such as railroads or airlines, and you notice that the Dow Jones Transportation Index begins to show a downward trend over a period of time, you may want to reevaluate your positions in those transportation stocks. While your specific investments may or may not be part of the index itself, you can use the index as a gauge by which to determine the market's general attitude toward transportation stocks. Sometimes certain market sectors are either in favor or out of favor with investors, meaning that investments in those sectors are viewed either positively or negatively at the time, for any number of reasons. It is certainly to your advantage to be invested in sectors that are in favor, because the market's positive attitude about that sector is likely to affect all stocks in the sector.

Interpreting the Indexes

Reading the data in the market indexes is similar to reading a stock table. One of the best sources for information on the performance of the market indexes is *The Wall Street Journal,* but other financial newspapers and magazines make this information available as well. Each day, the performance of a number of indexes is reported in a table that looks like this:

Major Indexes

High	Low	(12-MO)	Close	Net Chg	% Chg	12-MO Chg	% Chg	From 12/31	% Chg
Dow Jones Averages									
6560.91	5032.94	30 Industrials	6448.27	−101.10	−1.54	+1270.82	+24.55	+1331.15	+26.01
2315.47	1882.71	20 Transport	2255.67	−24.97	−1.09	+255.30	+12.76	+274.67	+13.87
238.12	204.86	15 Utilities	232.53	−2.59	−1.10	+5.10	+2.24	+7.13	+3.16
2059.18	1655.55	65 Composite	2025.83	−28.15	−1.37	+314.35	+18.37	+332.62	+19.64

The tables printed in *The Wall Street Journal* will list not only the Dow Jones Averages, as in the previous example, but also the other major indexes such as the New York Stock Exchange indexes, the Standard & Poor's indexes, the Nasdaq indexes, and other indexes such as the Russell 2000 and the Wilshire 5000.

RECORDS ARE MADE TO BE BROKEN

It took over 100 years, but the Dow Jones Industrial Average hit a milestone of 10,000 in 1999. While Wall Streeters were still cheering, the Dow hit 11,000 just a few months later, leaving the 10,000 record to gather dust. Other records have been made, broken, and broken again in the initial public offering (IPO) arena. The largest domestic IPO in 1998 was $4.40 billion by oil company Conoco, Inc., but it was soon surpassed by UPS in 1999 at $7.46 billion, and again by the $10.6 billion of AT&T Wireless in 2000. Italy's state-owned electric utility ENEL went public in 1999 with a total offering of $18.9 billion, creating the largest IPO ever. As of this writing (and so far this millennium), these records still stand. No doubt, other record-breakers are around the corner.

The first thing you'll notice in this table is how similar it is to a stock table. The numbers include high and low prices for the year, the closing price for the day, and the amount of increase the index experienced from the previous day. Reading the table from left to right, the first bit of information you will see is the 365-day high and low for that index. These columns give you a good idea of the historical performance of the index over the past year. The next column displays the name of the index, and just to the right of that, you'll see the closing figure of that index for that particular day, followed by the net change in the index as compared to the previous day and the percentage change that the net change represents.

The indexes are calculated every day that the market is open, so you can track the performance of these indexes daily, if you wish. The Dow Jones Industrial Average is probably the most widely followed index, with the daily closing figure announced on nearly every television and radio news broadcast on every channel in the country. Whether or not this index should be the most important one for you to watch is not a given, however. As you learn more about the specific industries tracked by the different indexes, you'll be able to determine which ones are most relevant to your own investments.

The next column is the 365-day change, which represents the amount that the index has changed compared to the same day one year ago. This is also expressed in the next column as a percentage change. The final two columns of the table represent the year-to-date change (as measured from the previous year end) in the index, expressed both as a numeric change as well as a percentage change. These last four columns, as well as the first two columns (those indicating the 365-day high and low figures) are extremely helpful for investors to determine current market trends. If the current closing figures, for example, are close to the 365-day high or low, you can see whether the general trend in the market is up or down.

You can also use these figures as benchmarks against which to measure your own investment performance. If the market trends are generally upward, but your own investment portfolio is down significantly, you may want to reassess your investments to determine why you are lagging behind the general market. While you can't always expect to mirror the performance of the market as a whole, understanding how your investments are doing in comparison to the rest of the investing world is helpful.

Specific Indexes and What They Track

Now that you have a basic understanding of what the indexes are and what they are used for, you can start to look at some of the specific indexes and averages that are commonly tracked. While it can be instructive to consider the performance of the Dow Jones Average, for example, that index may not be particularly relevant to your specific investment goals or portfolio, simply because you may be invested in different markets or sectors than those tracked by the Dow. That said, however, it is helpful to understand that the trends that the indexes exhibit sometimes follow similar patterns across all markets. If the Dow is up on a given day, therefore, it is also possible that the Nasdaq Composite will be up, because the positive investor sentiment that moved the Dow up probably influenced the other market sectors as well. While this interaction among the indexes is generally true, it is not a given fact, so you will benefit by knowing which index or average most closely reflects your own investment portfolio.

The Dow Jones Industrial Average

The Dow is the most popular and widely followed measurement of the performance of the stock market, in large part because it is the oldest and most consistently reported

"The Dow" 30

The now famous Dow averages are calculated to help investors gauge the overall strength or weakness of the American economy. They are given in three primary indexes: the Industrial Average, the Transportation Average, and the Utilities Average.

These are the companies used to compile the index you most often hear about, the Dow Jones Industrial Average:

Alcoa	IBM
American Express	Intel
AT&T	International Paper
Boeing	Johnson & Johnson
Caterpillar	J.P. Morgan
Citigroup	McDonalds
Coca-Cola	Merck & Company
DuPont	Microsoft
Eastman Kodak	Minnesota Mining & Manufacturing
Exxon/Mobil	Philip Morris
General Electric	Proctor & Gamble
General Motors	SBC Communications
Hewlett-Packard	United Technologies
Home Depot	Wal-Mart Stores
Honeywell International	Walt Disney

index used today. This average is comprised of 30 stocks of some of the largest and most successful companies in America.

The Dow Jones Average is considered the granddaddy of indexes, but in recent years analysts have begun to question whether it is an accurate indicator of the state of the market and the overall economy. In fact, the Dow is a good indicator of the performance of 30 very specific, very large-capitalization companies. Because the stocks in the index are large-cap stocks, the Dow may also serve as a good indicator of the market's general attitude toward other large-cap stocks that fall into the same category as the companies in the index. However, regardless of whether the Dow is in fact an accurate indicator of the health of the markets and the economy, it is widely thought to be such an indicator, and it is therefore important for investors to consider.

The companies included in the Dow Jones Industrial Average are some of the biggest companies in America. And while they all come from different sectors of the market-place, the index is clearly weighted toward industrial companies that manufacture and sell products to various markets. But suppose you were interested in investing primarily in utilities companies. Would the Dow Industrials give you a good indicator of how that sector is performing? Probably not. Or suppose you were primarily invested in transportation companies. Again, the Dow 30 might not necessarily be the best indicator of the performance of that market segment. Two other indexes would be useful, however: the Dow Jones Utilities Average and the Dow Jones Transportation Average.

The Dow Jones Utilities Average

This index tracks the performance of 15 companies that specialize in the creation and delivery of energy to American industry as well as the American public. These companies provide electricity, nat-

DOW UTILITIES

The 15 companies that comprise this index are:

American Electric Power
Columbia Energy Group
Consolidated Edison, Inc.
Dominion Resources
Duke Energy
Edison International
Enron Reliant Energy
PECO Energy
Pacific Gas and Electric
Public Service Enterprise
   Group
Southern Co.
TXU Corporation
Unicom
Williams Cos.

ural gas, oil, and other forms of energy, which are used to power the manufacture of just about any industrial product, as well as the heat and light used in homes and apartments throughout the country. These companies, like the companies tracked by the Industrial Average, are formidable representatives of the American corporate scene. The index is a good indicator of the strength of the utilities sector for any period of time.

The Dow Jones Transportation Average

Like the Dow Jones Utilities Average, the Transportation Average tracks the performance of companies in a specific sector of the marketplace. In this case, the companies that comprise the index are large-capitalization companies that provide transportation services to other industries and to the general public. These companies include railroads, trucking companies, and airlines and are among the largest transportation companies in the country. Their performance, as measured by the Dow Jones Transportation Average, is a good indicator of the health and overall strength of the transportation services sector of the American economy.

For more information about Dow Jones & Company and the indexes it maintains, visit the Dow Jones Web site: <www.dowjones.com>.

The Standard & Poor's 500 Index

The three primary indexes produced and maintained by Dow Jones & Company are probably the most popular and often consulted market indexes today. They provide benchmarks for three very important sectors of the American economy: industry, utilities, and transportation. But these indexes tend to be biased in favor of only a few very large-capitalization companies. While these indexes may be good indicators of their respective market sectors as far as large companies are concerned, they neglect to consider the economic impact and strength of many of the smaller, often more dynamic, companies, which are driving economic change and growth. For this reason, other indexes were created in attempts to provide broader-based measurements that consider both small-cap and large-cap companies.

The most popular of these broader-based indexes is the Standard & Poor's 500 index (the S&P 500). This index is based on a selection of 500 representative stocks from a

wider range of market sectors than those represented by the Dow Jones averages.

In addition, the S&P 500 takes into consideration companies with a broader range of market capitalization than those in the Dow averages. For example, the smallest-cap company in the S&P 500 has a market capitalization of about $470 million, while the largest-cap company in the index has a market capitalization of about $524 billion. This wide range of companies from varying sectors often is thought to provide a better indicator of the general strength of the stock market as well as the national economy as a whole.

Another difference between the S&P 500 and the Dow Jones indexes is that the S&P 500 is a weighted index. This simply means that the stocks that are used in the index are given different weight in the overall index based on the market value of the company. The net effect of this weighting is that companies with greater market capitalization will have more of an influence upon the overall index than those with lower capitalization. While this weighting may seem unfair at first glance, it is an accurate reflection of the larger economy, because larger companies generally have a greater impact upon the economy than smaller ones.

MORE DOW

The Dow Transportation Average is comprised of the following 20 stocks:

AMR
Airborne Freight
Alexander & Baldwin
Burlington Northern
   Santa Fe
CNF Transportation
CSX Corporation
Delta Air Lines
Federal Express
GATEX Corporation
J.B. Hunt Transportation
Norfolk Southern
Northwest Airlines
Roadway Express
Ryder System
Southwest Airlines
UAL
Union Pacific
USAir Group
US Freightways
Yellow

The complete list of stocks in the S&P 500 is too large to put in this book, but you can find them all on the S&P Web site < www.spglobal.com >. The composition of the index in terms of the distribution of stocks in different sectors is a great way to consider the range of companies included in this index. According to the Standard & Poor's Web site, the current breakdown of the S&P 500 index in terms of representation by industry group is as follows:

Sector	No. of Companies	% of 500	Market Value as % of 500
Industrials	378	75.6	80.28
Utilities	40	8.0	3.29
Financials	71	14.2	15.82
Transportation	11	2.2	.61
	500	100.0	100.00

As you can see, although the distribution of stocks in the S&P 500 is heavily weighted toward the industrial sector, the total number of companies included in even the smallest represented sector is about as many as the total number of companies represented in the entire Dow Jones Utilities Average. The S&P 500 also includes the financial services sector, which is not included in any of the Dow Jones averages. This broad range of information makes the S&P 500 one of the most useful and informative indexes available for investors in all markets.

The Russell 2000

The S&P 500 presents a good, wide-ranging index based on evaluations of stocks from a broad base of companies with a variety of market capitalizations. If, however, you are primarily interested in investing in small-capitalization companies, the S&P 500 may not be the best measurement for you to consider because it includes some very large-capitalization stocks. The S&P may be the best overall benchmark of the market as a whole, but for small-cap stocks, the most widely used measure is the Russell 2000. The Russell 2000 is comprised of the 2,000 lowest-capitalization stocks in the Russell 3000, which is made up of the 3,000 largest-capitalization stocks in the entire U.S. stock market. The average market capitalization of the Russell 2000 stocks is about $420 million, with the largest capitalization being just over $1 billion.

As you can see, this index serves the purpose of providing a good standard for investors who are primarily attracted to smaller-capitalization stocks, which may have better potential for high growth than some of the larger, more established companies. These indexes, and a host of other, similar Russell indexes are created and maintained by the Frank Russell Company. For more information, including definitions of all the Russell indexes, visit the Frank Russell Company's Web site <www.russell.com>.

The NYSE Composite Index

The New York Stock Exchange also maintains a series of indexes that reflect the performance of all stocks that trade on the NYSE. The NYSE actually maintains five indexes, all based on the performance of the stocks traded on that exchange. The most frequently consulted of these is the NYSE Composite Index. This index is made up of all the common stocks listed on the New York Stock Exchange. While this composite index does not take market sectors or capitalization into account, it is a very representative index of the performance of the broader market, because the NYSE is the largest and most active stock exchange in the world.

In addition to the composite index, the NYSE maintains four sector-based indexes. These indexes reflect the same business sectors as those that make up the S&P 500: industrials, utilities, transportation, and finance. Again, these indexes are based on all the stocks in their respective business sectors that trade on the NYSE, but because of the influence and importance of this exchange, these indexes can be very useful measures of the economic condition of the entire market.

The Nasdaq and AMEX Indexes

The Nasdaq stock market and the American Stock Exchange (AMEX) also manage indexes relating to their specific markets. The AMEX maintains an index called the AMEX Market Value Index, which measures all the stocks (about 800 at present)

A SEAT ON THE EXCHANGE

When you become a tremendously successful investor, racking up profits as consistently as Tiger Woods wins PGA events, you may decide it's time to get serious about this business and skip the commissions and brokers and everyone else standing between you and pure profits and buy a seat on the New York Stock Exchange.

While you may be able to afford the sheer cost of buying an exchange seat, you may still have a hard time getting one. The NYSE and the AMEX are private associations with a limited number of memberships available. For example, the NYSE has 1,366 members, while the AMEX has 661. On the other hand, if the markets are in turmoil and stocks are consistently losing ground, you may be able to get a seat at a reasonable cost. But the question is, would you really want one?

What Is a Market "Crash"?

Everyone has heard of the "crash of 1929" and the "crash of 1987," but what does *crash* actually mean?

A market crash is an unusually large drop in the overall value of the stock market that occurs on a particular day. The reasons for a crash are usually a combination of overvalued stocks and a lagging or problematic economy. If you consider the trends in the market in the six months preceding the crashes of 1929 and 1987, you'll see very similar patterns of rapidly rising prices ending ultimately in a precipitous drop on a particular day.

After both crashes, the government implemented measures to attempt to ward off crashes in the future by regulating the markets when prices drop rapidly. For example, in the wake of the 1929 crash, the government passed legislation known as The Securities Act of 1933 to regulate the markets and presumably to forestall market crashes in the future. In addition, the Securities and Exchange Commission was created in 1934 to help enforce these and other securities laws.

After the 1987 crash, a number of measures were instituted to further regulate computerized trading, which had contributed greatly to the sell-off in that year. New "circuit breakers" rules went into effect in 1998 that halt trading when the Dow Jones Industrial Average falls 10, 20, or 30 percent. These measures hopefully will prevent such radical crashes in the value of the stock market in the future, although the markets aren't guaranteed not to drop in value over the course of a number of days or weeks.

traded on the AMEX. The Nasdaq stock market, like the NYSE, manages both a composite index as well as sector-specific indexes. However, the sectors tracked in the Nasdaq indexes are different than those tracked by the NYSE indexes or the S&P 500. The Nasdaq indexes include industrials, insurance, technology, and banking. Because of the differences in composition in the stocks traded by the various markets and exchanges, learning which index relates most closely to your personal investing style and portfolio is to your benefit. If you are heavily invested in insurance and banking stocks, for example, the Nasdaq sector indexes might be better sources for you than the Dow Jones averages or the S&P 500.

The Wilshire 5000

The Wilshire 5000 is the broadest index of all, encompassing all stocks traded both over-the-counter and on the exchanges. This index tracks all stocks for which daily price quotations are readily available. While this index currently does not garner as much attention as the Dow Jones averages or the S&P 500, it is the most representative of the entire marketplace because it includes all quoted stocks.

Other Indexes

The indexes discussed thus far are the most widely available indexes, with their values published daily in *The Wall Street Journal* and other financial newspapers nationwide. But they are not the only indexes used to track the performance of the stock market. Hundreds of indexes track the performance of all sorts of business sectors, market capitalizations, and stock exchanges. In addition to indexes that track the U.S. stock markets, other indexes measure the activities of the bond markets, precious metals markets, and commodities such as oil and gas, as well as all the international stock

HOW MUCH DOES A SEAT COST?

The price of a seat on the NYSE is determined by the laws of supply and demand. When stocks are going through a bear market, demand typically drops, and the price drops. The highest price ever paid for a seat on the NYSE was $2.65 million in 1999. The lowest price ever paid was $4,000 in 1876 and 1878. The lowest price ever paid for a seat during the twentieth century was $17,000 in 1942.

exchanges and every conceivable subset thereof. Indexes have proliferated so widely and become so entrenched in the markets that they are no longer solely used as indicators but are also used as the basis of investment vehicles like futures and index funds (mutual funds that invest in all the stocks in an index in order to mirror their performance).

Other, less commonly referenced indexes are out there, too. You can contact the companies that maintain them or search for information on the World Wide Web:

- Nasdaq 100 Index

- S&P 400 MidCap Stock Index

- S&P 100 Stock Index

- PSE Technology Index

COULD YOU AFFORD TO LOSE THIS MUCH?

Until the big surges and dives of the latter part of the 20th century, Ray Kroc, chairman of McDonald's, had the distinction of losing the largest amount of stock market equity—$65 million on July 8, 1974. Since then, even bigger investors have had even bigger losses— hundreds of millions of dollars in the 1990s. Just ask Bill Gates of Microsoft—his portfolio took a $33 billion hit in April of 2000.

- Morgan Stanley High Technology 35 Index

- AMEX Computer Technology Index

- Wilshire Small Cap Index

- Financial Times Stock Exchange Index

- Toronto 35 Index

- TSE 100 Index

- TSE 300 Composite Index

- Mexico's IPC Stock Index

- PHLX Gold and Silver Index

- AMEX Oil & Gas Index

- Value Line Index

- Russell 1000 Index

While the sheer number of indexes can be overwhelming, sticking with the most common indexes (like those explained in this chapter) will give you enough of a grasp on the overall performance of the stock market and its various component sectors so that you'll never be at a loss to know how the markets are doing on a day-to-day basis.

BEARS AND BULLS

A bull market refers to a period of time when the overall market averages are trending upward, whereas a bear market is a period of time when the markets are on a downward cycle. Why bulls and bears? Bulls evoke images of bullfights and rodeos, sports that feature powerful, charging beasts moving forward despite any obstacles. Bears, on the other hand, make you think of big, furry critters all curled up in hibernation. A bull market gets its name from the potent forward charge of growth that drives it, but a bear market is usually marked by declining stocks or, often, long-term, sleepy markets during which nothing seems to move upward at all.

BIG
plans
for many
happy
RETURNS

CHAPTER SIX

*Now that you've got a handle on how the **market works** and understand stock charts, tables, and indexes like the back of your hand, and you can distinguish a **good broker** from a shyster a mile away, it's time to consider a few **investment strategies.***

It's one thing to understand the principles of the stock market in theory, but it's quite another to take that knowledge and transform it into profits for your investments.

Instead of merely following larger market trends or buying stock in your favorite restaurant, you can use a number of fairly reliable methods to pick winners. If you can, for example, outsmart the Dow Jones Industrial Average or the S&P 500 by pulling in consistent returns that beat those indexes, you'll be among the top 25 percent of all professional money managers who spend their careers managing mutual funds. A couple of the methods you'll read about later promise to help you deliver those kinds of returns, but your own performance will vary, and there are definitely no guarantees.

In this chapter, you'll get a look at some of the most interesting and effective stock-picking strategies that have ever been conceived. You'll read about the geniuses that came up with these ideas, learn about how to implement them in your own investments, and find out where to get more information about each one, straight from the source. If you are willing to do a little basic math, you'll be able to track the numbers on some of these strategies—and you'll discover that they're solid, tested investment methods, which can help you turn an average portfolio into a stellar one.

While some of these strategies may seem to contradict each other, remember that there's more than one way to skin a cat. You need to weigh the pros and cons of these various alternatives to see which technique best fits your personal investing style and your investment goals. But once you've chosen a method, don't feel that you're locked in. If a particular strategy doesn't fit, you can always try another one. Finally, get your hands on some of the books you'll read about here. These investment classics should be in every investor's library of invaluable references on how to make good in the stock market.

What Is Risk?

Before you sink even one dime into the stock market, you need to come to terms with the fact that any investment strategy, from the most aggressive to the most benign, involves a certain measure of risk. You need to understand that you can lose money in the market nearly as easily as you can make money. For every dollar you invest in stocks, you have to accept that at the end of the year, you may not get back a dollar and a quarter—in fact, you may get back only $.75. Because the markets are volatile and rather irrational, risk is always associated with investing, even with the safest stocks you can find.

What are some of the specific risks that can cause you to lose money? One of the most obvious is that the stock you purchase may not perform well in the market. Even if you've researched and investigated the stock thoroughly, it may not go up in price. A number of factors could cause this. Your timing may have been wrong. You may have purchased the shares of your stock when it had just completed an abrupt upswing in price. When the market lets the price relax a bit after this run-up, you might panic as you watch your investment lose 5 to 10 percent of its value over a couple of weeks.

Whether the price goes up or down after you sell is irrelevant; you've already lost because your timing was off and you either sold too soon or bought too late. Timing the market for profits is one of the most difficult strategies to follow. It helps to learn to be patient, regardless of whether you've got a long-term or a short-term outlook.

Another potential cause of losses is a market correction or crash. While no one likes to think about crashes, sometimes they happen, and they tend to catch most people off guard. A market correction, while less severe than a crash, often occurs even during bull markets. If the market has been climbing steadily for some time without a drop in price, investors tend to get nervous about the possibility that stocks are overpriced and therefore due for a correction to bring their prices down to a more reasonable level. Sometimes this very tension brings about a correction, but sometimes the stocks really are overvalued and need to be brought back into a reasonable price range. These market corrections are unpredictable, as every investor has a different perspective on what a stock's fair value might be at any particular time. Corrections, like crashes, tend to be distinct events that occur on particular days or over the course of just a few days. They're often followed by a renewed vigor in the markets, and then again, sometimes they aren't.

For example, if you invest during a bear market (a period of time when stocks in general are out of favor and losing value across the board), you're likely to experience a decrease in share value simply because the entire market is losing value for a prolonged period of time. Bear markets typically occur in periods of general economic decline, so you might have a better chance of predicting the continuation of a bear market than the specific occurrence of a correction or crash. But if you do invest during a bear market without realizing it, you're not likely to experience capital gains on your investments. Some stocks increase in value even during bear markets, because some companies will find ways of bringing in profits even when the general economy is weak. But profits are hard to find when the bears are on the loose.

Penny Stocks and Blue Chips

Another risk you may face in your investments is inherent in the types of stocks you're attracted to. The quality of stocks ranges from the relative safety and security of some of the biggest, most profitable companies in America, to the iffiness companies of

extremely questionable lineage, which may not even have the financial wherewithal to survive until the week after you put your money into them. Stocks in the large, stable companies are called blue chips, and they get this moniker from poker, where the blue chips have the greatest value. Stocks in less solid companies are known as penny stocks, so-called because you can usually buy shares of these companies for pennies on the dollar. A wide range of corporate value is available on the scale, from penny stocks to blue chips, so you usually can find something sound yet affordable, with growth potential to boot.

All this scary talk about the perils of investing isn't meant to frighten you away from assuming some calculated risk in the stock market. An interesting correlation exists between the amount of risk people are willing to take and the amount of reward that they can reasonably expect to gain. While the blue chip stocks are probably among the safest investments you can make in any market, the gain you can achieve from these dinosaurs is typically on the low side, because they are already enormous corporations with little room to grow. Corporate growth makes a stock's price appreciate over time. So, while you stand a greater chance of losing your investment by purchasing the stock of lower-priced or smaller companies, because they are less solid and stable than their blue-blooded cousins, you also stand a better chance of making greater profits if those small companies grow into big companies. And although investing in true penny stocks (the lowest of the low-priced stocks, companies that perhaps shouldn't even have stock outstanding at all) is probably not only excessively risky but possibly even a bit on the dumb side, you can always find stocks of small, profitable companies that are on a growth trajectory and could yield significant gains over time.

Buy Low, Sell High

The greatest technique of all time for making huge amounts of money in the stock market is summed up in four very little but very powerful words: buy low, sell high. You need learn no other techniques, read no other books, and heed no other advice. If you can consistently buy low and sell high, you know all there is to know to make it on Wall Street.

The problem is to find a way to be able to buy low, sell high often enough to come out ahead at the end of all your transactions, rather than behind. So while buy low, sell high is the consummate investor's wisdom, the strategy to end all strategies, abiding by this maxim all the time isn't that easy. But that's where all the other investing strategies come in.

Value Investing

Strategy number one is commonly known as the value method of investing. It's also known as investing on the basis of fundamentals, or fundamental analysis. All those things you learned in chapter three about numbers, balance sheets, income statements, and the like are the tools of the trade for fundamental investors, because investing in fundamentals means investing in stocks on the basis of the value of the companies behind those stocks. This strategy requires knowledge and patience, but it may be the very best investment strategy you can find. The value, or fundamental analysis, strategy is used by investors like Peter Lynch and Warren Buffett, two of the most successful investors in history. Fundamental analysis is also recommended by the National Association of Investors Corporation (NAIC), the association that includes investing clubs such as The Beardstown Ladies' Investment Club.

When you use the fundamental analysis strategy, you learn as much as possible about the financial and market position of a company, then determine from those fundamentals whether or not the company's future prospects appear promising. If your analysis of the historical growth and profit patterns of the company shows a steadily growing organization, and your research indicates that the company's management is sound and competent, fundamental analysis concludes that you have good reason to believe the company will continue its positive growth momentum into the future.

A value investor tries to find companies that have solid fundamentals and that display promise for continuing those strong numbers into the future. Part of the job is discovering companies that may be undervalued by the markets, and the other part involves holding on to those stocks for the long run, without getting scared off by occasional short-term dips in the price of the stock.

What Constitutes Value?

Value is defined differently by different people, so no single, foolproof way exists to ensure the stocks you are buying are the best value stocks you can find. A number of indicators, however, can help you determine the fair value of a stock: price-to-

earnings (PE) ratio, the price-to-book ratio, and the price-to-sales ratio. While none of these indicators should be taken into consideration as the sole means of valuing a company, they can be useful when considered together and with other indicators like indexes.

For example, if you're buying into small-capitalization companies, the Russell 2000 might help you determine how the company in which you're interested compares with other companies in the same industry. You may also want to compare the stock performance of other similar companies to determine their market value and thereby get a better sense of how the market values those types of companies in general. As you invest more over time, you'll begin to develop your own sense of what a company's fair value should be. Until then, study as many indicators as you can and try to use your common sense. If a stock has a PE ratio of 175 but the corporation has been losing money hand over fist for the past year, you probably aren't in the company of a stock you really want to be friends with over the long haul.

Finding Sound Companies

So how do you find these fundamentally sound companies that will grow and grow into great future profits? To borrow from Peter Lynch, one great way to find fundamentally sound companies is to invest in what you know. Lynch is a great advocate of what might be called the intelligent and observant consumer. According to Mr. Lynch, the average person has an advantage over even the most savvy and tuned-in Wall Street analyst, because the average person can spot trends in businesses before Wall Street even gets wind of their existence.

A great example is Wal-Mart. In the early days, before the company became a retailing megagiant and a household name, Wal-Mart stores were opening quietly for business in many small communities across the country. Not that the opening of a new business in the neighborhood is itself enough to be a stock tip, but the opening of a new business that is constantly crowded with eager and enthusiastic shoppers is altogether another story. If you happened to be an average American shopper who was looking for good deals on merchandise and you happened to walk into a crowded Wal-Mart in those early days, you were standing right smack in the middle of one of the best stock tips anyone anywhere could ever give you. And success stories like Wal-Mart are opening up in communities across the country on a daily basis.

As a shrewd investor, you have to keep your eyes open for these situations, and when you spot something that looks promising, call the company or do a little research on the Internet. If the fundamentals are positive and match your observations of local success in your area, you just might be on to something exciting.

The Beardstown Ladies' Investment Club spells out another method for finding promising investments. In their book, *The Beardstown Ladies' Common-Sense Investment Guide,* they strongly suggest using *The Value Line Investment Survey* as a primary investor's tool to ferret out attractive and fundamentally sound stocks. *The Value Line* ranks companies on the basis of several proprietary measures, such as industry ranking, timeliness, and safety. In addition, *The Value Line* offers historical pricing information, information about trading volumes, and summary analyses of the company's prospects by a professional stock analyst. The Beardstown Ladies recommend a ten-point investment approach, which only selects stocks ranked in the highest categories of safety, timeliness, and industry ranking. They also encourage investors to be sure that the company's debt is low and that the earnings are positive and expected to grow over time. A low PE ratio is also considered a positive indicator in this model, although the PE ratio may not necessarily be the best overall indicator—a PE ratio that is high for one company and one set of circumstances may be low for another company under different conditions. *The Value Line* tracks over a thousand stocks on a regular basis, so you'll have plenty of possible companies to choose from as you pour through the available information. *The Value Line* is available by subscription, but you can find copies of this invaluable guide in most public libraries.

The final element of the fundamental analysis strategy is time. When you've made your selections of fundamentally strong companies, you have to be willing to put your money into those companies for a long period of time in order to profit from their growth. This strategy is generally profitable over the course of years, not necessarily weeks or months. The stock market will always experience ups and downs in the short run, but over the long term, stocks of quality companies rise with the fortunes of those companies.

You always have to keep an eye on your investments to make sure the companies you initially selected still meet your criteria of fundamental value. If you buy shares of stock in a company that starts losing money or market share, you may have to reevaluate

your investment and move your money into another, more promising alternative. However, if the companies you invest in on the basis of value analysis continue to grow and prosper, your stocks generally will do the same.

Market Timing

The strategy that stands at the opposite end of the spectrum from the value or fundamental analysis approach is the approach that tries to gauge the short-term swings of the market. This strategy can be profitable, but it requires making rapid decisions and having extraordinarily good timing. If you are unable to make snap judgments to buy or sell a stock at a moment's notice and for a gain, perhaps, of only a fraction of a point per share, the market timing strategy is not for you. Because of the short-term volatility of the stock market, investors can make money on short-term price fluctuations. But the risks here are great, your timing must be impeccable, and you may have to invest in great quantities of stock to eke out profits from eighth-of-a-point movements on a minute-by-minute basis.

Market timing methods range from those of day traders, who try to take advantage of daily or hourly price changes to make a profit, to somewhat longer-term investors, who try to time stock price movements over the course of a few days or even weeks on the basis of various trends they've noticed in the stock's recent performance. While both market timing strategies have similar charac-

THE TREND IS YOUR FRIEND

You not only need to keep an eye on your investments and their performance in your own portfolio, but also on the pricing trends for that stock and the trends in the marketplace overall.

If, for example, you notice an upward trend in a particular stock, you may want to purchase shares of that stock if all other factors relating to the company are positive. But if that stock is out of favor and on a downward trend, you may consider avoiding it, at least for the time being.

You should try to buy stocks as they're rising to new highs and not when they're dropping down to new lows. If the overall market is down and most stocks are dropping, be extra careful. While it is certainly possible to profit during bear markets, you'll have a harder time finding profitable stocks when the market as a whole is dropping in value.

Types of Risk

Risk is an unavoidable fact of life for investors in any kind of savings or investment plan. And every type of risk can have a different effect on your portfolio.

Market risk affects nearly all investors, whether their money is in stocks, bonds, or even bank savings accounts. The market as a whole might possibly tank at any time. If the market overall drops in value significantly, as it did in 1929, most investors wind up losing at least some of the value of their investments.

Interest rate risk affects bond investors more than stock investors as a general rule. If interest rates rise, bond prices drop. If interest rates drop, bond prices go up. While at times bonds may seem to be safe investment vehicles, bond investors are always concerned about interest rates.

Credit risk affects bonds more than other types of investments. The issuer of the bonds you purchased may not be able to keep up with interest payments. Or worse, the issuer might not be able to pay back even the original principle of the investment. While bondholders usually get paid back before stockholders if a company goes out of business, bondholders are not guaranteed to get their investments back if the company simply runs out of money.

Currency risk primarily affects international investors and currency speculators. Because currency exchange rates fluctuate daily, changes in these rates can adversely influence investments in foreign stocks or currency. For example, if you own stocks of successful British companies and the dollar is very strong compared to the pound, because of the unfavorable exchange rate, your investments will turn out to have less value should you choose to cash in your shares.

Economic risk affects nearly all investors if the economy experiences a general decline. During the depression era of the early 1930s, many countries had economic difficulties, which made most people's investments lose a great deal of value.

Manager risk affects mutual fund investors. Suppose you buy shares of a fund at $10 per share, and because of incompetence or lack of experience, the fund manager loses money on all the investments. In this unfortunate case, your mutual fund would end up losing you a great deal of money.

Inflation risk, the dwindling value of money over time, is perhaps the most subtle and pernicious of all risks. If inflation is at an average rate of 3 percent per year, your investments have to earn at least 3 percent annually for you (after taxes) to ensure that your money doesn't lose value because of inflation. So socking away your dollars under a mattress isn't such a great way to save for the future. If you aren't at least keeping up with the rate of inflation year after year, the value of your money will continue to decrease.

teristics, they differ fundamentally in that the day trader tries to squeeze profits from very small, momentary price movements, whereas the longer-term market timer tries to take advantage of trends in the recent price movement of a stock.

If you've ever watched a Quotron flash across the bottom of the TV screen on one of those all-news-all-the-time cable stations, you've seen how the price of any given stock fluctuates as it trades throughout the day. You may even have had the passing fancy that if you could buy 1,000 shares of some stock in the morning, then sell it later that day for a gain of a quarter or an eighth of a point, you could make a nice little chunk of money in very little period of time. Multiply that $100 or $200 gain by ten transactions a day, and you may be looking at thousands of dollars in short-term investing profits.

Or at least that's the theory. But the fact is that, more often than not, the stock price swings downward by an eighth, so that at the end of the day you're still stuck holding on to a stock that didn't quite perform as expected. If that stock drops another eighth the next day, you'll be a buy-and-hold investor of that particular stock before you can blink and say, "Capital gains!" The day-trading strategy is not for the faint of heart, nor is it for those who can't do enough math to figure out exactly how much they need to make on a transaction to cover commissions (you definitely don't want to use a full-service broker if you're into day trading) and the inevitable taxes all those little trades will generate. The key to success in this approach, as in any other, is consistency. You have to be able to make little profits on a daily basis that can cover your commissions and leave you with a little more money in your pocket after each trade.

The market timer who tries to take advantage of somewhat longer-term market volatility is often looking for stocks that may be on a short-term upswing because of a rumor or a positive piece of news. For example, plenty of companies buy other companies every year so they can expand their market share or even move into niches or markets that they haven't yet been able to tap into successfully on their own. Those who are lucky enough to be on the trading floor of the NYSE are in a position to hear about potential buyouts or mergers. But most of us can't afford to be there, so we have to settle for the next best thing: the Internet, one of the greatest rumor mills in the world, where you can get wind of takeovers from the comfort of your living room or office.

Novell (NOVL) is a great example. For years, it was rumored to be a takeover candidate by the much larger IBM. In fact, at the end of 1995, NOVL stock had a run from about $12 per share to about $18 in the course of a week, because the rumors of the takeover really sounded good. The stock dropped right back down the next week because the rumor turned out to have no basis in reality, but if you could have timed your purchase of NOVL on the basis of these speculations, you'd have made a 50 percent return within a week.

While it may appear in hindsight that certain stock purchases could have been timed wonderfully for great short-term gains, this method is probably the most risky and the most unreliable method of investing that you'll ever encounter. For example, suppose you bought NOVL at $16 on the basis of those "really reliable" rumors and you hung on to that stock expecting it to hit $20. You may even have believed that the rumors were really onto something, so you figured there was no way to lose. But that one week when the stock went from $12 to $18 and then back down again was a very short period of time. By the time you might have figured out that the rumor had no basis, you'd have lost $4 a share as the stock settled back down to $12.

Market timing is extremely difficult to do consistently because accurately predicting the future movement of any stock's price is impossible. How is market timing different from predicting upward price movement for a stock based on fundamental analysis? The answer is history. If you study the history of the stock market, you'll notice that over all the years, without fail, strong companies with strong earnings usually appreciate in value over the long term. While these companies may occasionally have setbacks, and the market may crash or experience a correction that affects these stocks in the short term, over the years strong companies will have strong stock values.

So what information do market timers use to try to work their magic? One tactic is to use what is known as technical analysis. This analysis is different from fundamental analysis, because whereas the fundamentals are concerned primarily with the strength of the underlying corporation, technical analysis is concerned strictly with the patterns that appear on a stock's historical price chart. In other words, it attempts to use the historical pattern of a stock's price movement to predict the future of that stock's price movement. The theory is that certain patterns of stock prices tend to repeat themselves over time, regardless of the fundamental value of the underlying company. If you can

learn to spot these patterns, so the theory goes, you'll have a good chance of predicting short-term trends in the stock's price.

In addition to studying the chart of a specific stock, technical analysts also study trends in indexes and in the market's movement in general. These technical methods can be extremely complex, and complete software systems have been created to help technical analysts in spotting appropriate patterns. These methods are not stress-free, and many doubt their effectiveness. But if you think you've got the knack, you may be able to build a profitable portfolio with them.

C-A-N S-L-I-M

This strategy is a methodical approach to fundamental analysis investing. While using fundamental analysis to pick good companies is a great way to invest for the long term, you may be bothered by the nagging question of whether you've actually found a company that is a good value. The C-A-N S-L-I-M method proposes to answer that question very specifically. This method was created by William J. O'Neil, the founder of the financial newspaper, *Investor's Business Daily*. Mr. O'Neil is a highly regarded financial professional whose method and newspaper have helped many investors on the road to success. C-A-N S-L-I-M is an acronym that summarizes a basic, fundamental value philosophy for investing, created by one of the brightest minds in the financial industry after years of research. If you follow the seven principles of C-A-N S-L-I-M, you can, according to Mr. O'Neil's research, consistently outperform the stock market over the long term. This section will introduce you to a short summary of the C-A-N S-L-I-M method, but if you really want to dig in and learn more about it, you should consult Mr. O'Neil's book, *How to Make Money in Stocks*.

The first letter, *C*, refers to current earnings. Find stocks that show significant increases in earnings per share for the current quarter in comparison to the same quarter the previous year, because stocks of companies that show consistent and dramatic earnings increases tend to increase in value. Earnings relate to cash flow and income, and if these items on a company's balance sheet and income statement show positive figures that increase year to year, the company is a growing concern that should spark your investor's zeal for quality. Make sure, however, that the increase in earnings is steady and due to improvements in the company's business, not the result of a onetime or extra-

ordinary event like the sale of property or other assets. You are primarily interested in a company's growth on a quarter-by-quarter and year-by-year basis. Growing companies that are well managed are good investments.

The second letter of the formula, *A,* refers to annual earnings increases. In this case, you're more interested in looking at historical trends in the company's earnings pattern. You want to spot companies that have consistent growth over time. According to O'Neil, ideally you are searching for companies that have had increases in annual earnings per share each year for at least the past five years. This way, you're going to find companies that have a proven track record of regular and dependable growth over time, not flash-in-the-pan companies that show a great quarter in April but drop off like hot potatoes in July. The greatest key to a company's success is its earnings, so if a company can consistently produce positive earnings over time, that company is likely to be a winner. And the higher the percentage of growth, year after year, the better the stock.

The third letter, *N,* indicates that you should be looking for companies that have something new that makes them stand out from the crowd. Specifically, O'Neil indicates that the company should have new products, new management, or new highs in any combination or individually. Why new? Consider a company with a hot new product. A good example from recent years is Iomega Corporation (IOM). In early 1994, Iomega introduced a new kind of computer peripheral, the Zip

A RISING TIDE LIFTS ALL BOATS—OR DOES IT?

While following and keeping an eye on overall trends is a good way to know how your investments are doing relative to the general market, a rising market doesn't guarantee that all stocks will rise. While during a bull market more stocks rise than fall, you have to consider the trends surrounding each individual stock, too.

A great bull market will do nothing for a stock that is in financial trouble or losing market share. You have to consider industry trends and the pricing trends of specific stocks as well. Make sure you're investing in strong and reputable companies, even if the market as a whole is riding high on the wave of an incredible bull market. Lousy companies will have lousy stocks regardless of how the market is doing.

drive, which took the computing world by storm. This company had been lagging for a number of years and had teetered at the edge of bankruptcy for some of them. Then it introduced the Zip drive, a high-capacity, high-portability drive that allowed users to store large amounts of computer data inexpensively and efficiently. Not only did the Zip drive sell like hotcakes, but the company's stock went through the roof because of all the enthusiasm surrounding the product.

Or, consider a company with new management, like IBM. After a number of years of struggle and losses, IBM replaced its upper management with a new CEO who shook the company to its foundations. Lou Gerstner brought a fresh perspective to the ailing computer giant, and within a few years, he had turned the company around and had the stock price up over four times what it had been when he came on board.

Finally, look for companies whose stock price has reached new highs. While it may sound risky at an intuitive level to buy a stock that has hit a new high level of price, the fact is that stocks that are going up will break new highs as they continue their rise in price.

The letter *S* in the formula stands for supply and demand. The greater the number of shares outstanding, the harder it will be for the price to move up because investors will have to buy many more shares to cause the price to rise. The law of supply and demand indicates that if there is little supply but great demand for something, then the price of that thing will tend to rise. As an investor, your great advantage lies in finding companies that have as few shares outstanding as possible but whose daily trading volume is on the high side of high. If thousands of investors are clamoring to get in on the action of a particular stock, but there aren't that many shares to go around, the price is bound to rise to accommodate that demand.

L stands for leader or laggard. This is a key measure you have to apply to any company whose shares you are interested in buying. Is this company a leader in its industry, or does it lag behind others? When investing in stocks, you are absolutely, positively, and unfailingly interested in buying the leader. If you buy a lagging company's stock because you think that it will rise in sympathy with the success of the leading company, you will be sadly disappointed. The stock market is looking for winners, not also-rans. While the bronze medal may be an honorable achievement in the Olympics, in the stock market, the third-tier company in any industry is probably not going to be a

great investment. Consider Intel Corporation (INTC), a leader in the semiconductor industry. Intel is the leading manufacturer of computer chips (CPUs, or central processing units) for personal computers, with an estimated 80 percent of the market share for this type of equipment. As of this writing, Intel stock has managed to scale higher highs than any of its competitors' stocks have even come close to achieving. Why? Because this company is the undisputed leader in its market. Don't settle for less than a winner when you're investing your hard earned money.

I is for institutional sponsorship. An important consideration for the small investor, according to Mr. O'Neil, is whether or not the stock you are interested in buying has support from institutional investors, companies such as mutual funds and pension funds that have huge sums of money. When a stock attracts institutional investors, that stock is likely to go up in price because those institutions will have enough buying power to influence the price of the stock significantly. If a few such institutions are buying your favorite stock on a regular basis, you are likely to be swept up in the tide, as the price of that stock increases.

M stands for market direction. Here's where all your knowledge about indexes comes into play. While it is possible for a stock to increase in value during a bear market, generally speaking profiting from stocks when the market as a whole is negative is very difficult. Keep your eyes open to the trends in the overall marketplace, because the individual investor can buck those trends only with difficulty. If the market is heading down and appears to be on a long-term downward trend, you may want to consider parking your money in alternate investments like bonds or even cash investments, until the bears go back to sleep and the market appears to be picking up steam again.

C-A-N S-L-I-M is a very specific, seven-point approach to investing that can provide the basis for a profitable investment program for any investor, large or small. It's a clear-cut strategy, which gives you explicit parameters providing an invaluable framework upon which to base your buy and sell decisions.

The Miracle of DRIPs

Direct purchase programs, offered by many larger companies as part of their Dividend Reinvestment Programs (DRIPs), enable you to invest small amounts of money in some pretty big-time stocks without using a broker and without paying commissions.

These companies offer DRIPs to the public because they already have systems in place—the necessary legal and logistical requirements—to sell or offer stock directly to their employees.

If you purchase stocks through DRIPs, you can also buy odd lots of shares without paying an additional odd lot broker commission. A round lot is 100 shares, so if you're interested in buying stock that costs $150 a share, a round lot would be quite expensive, and if you ordered an odd lot, you might be hit with a higher transaction fee. But by taking advantage of DRIPs, you can buy any number of shares directly from the company without having to pay any commission at all.

While not all companies offer DRIPs, most larger companies, including many companies in the Dow Jones Industrial Average, offer these programs to investors. Companies offer DRIPs because DRIPs help stabilize the price of the company's stock by encouraging investors to hold their shares for longer periods. If more people hold stock longer, the share price tends to be less volatile because less trading activity is taking place on a day-to-day basis.

Why do DRIPs encourage longer-term holding? Because although buying stock directly from a company helps you save money on commissions and lets you buy smaller numbers of shares, these purchases require that you hold the shares in your own name. This requirement makes selling the shares when you decide it's time to cash in your stock somewhat more difficult, because you have to contact the administrator of the DRIP and send your stock certificates back to the company. The DRIP also designates certain days to sell your stock, so buying shares through a DRIP gives you somewhat less liquidity than purchasing shares on the open market through a broker.

Usually when you buy stock from a broker, the shares are held in "street name," meaning that the broker keeps the shares for your benefit in an account set aside for you. You usually don't receive certificates, and when you want to sell a position, you simply contact the broker and place the order. A DRIP makes selling your stock a bit more challenging, but this can benefit you by encouraging you to hang on to your shares for the long run.

The best way to learn about DRIPs is on the Internet by using one of the search engines (like Alta Vista or Yahoo!) to look for DRIPs. Or you can visit your local library

and use a resource like *The Value Line Investment Survey* to see if a company offers a DRIP. If you have a specific company in mind, you can contact it directly to see if they offer a Direct Purchase Program to the public. Taking advantage of DRIPs is one of the best ways to invest in solid companies while minimizing your expenses. You can start with a very small amount of money, so if you don't have enough stashed away to open a brokerage account, a DRIP may be the best way to start investing in stocks.

Beating the Dow

Michael O'Higgins is a highly respected money manager whose book, *Beating the Dow*, spells out a strategy that offers investors a low-risk way to outperform the market averages consistently. The method is based on the idea that among the 30 stocks of the Dow Jones Industrial Average (DJIA), some will always be out of favor at any given time. Historically, research indicates that stocks from this select group usually do better than the overall Dow Jones Average by a significant margin, yielding annual returns of 20 percent or more. While you can't judge future performance on the basis of what has happened in the past, O'Higgins' research is quite convincing. Even during bear markets like the ones witnessed in 1973 and 1974, this system has produced impressive returns year after year.

To determine which stocks are out of favor at any given time, O'Higgins recommends looking at the dividend yield of the Dow stocks and picking those with the combination of the lowest stock price along with the highest dividend yield. The dividend yield can be calculated by dividing the annual dividend by the current price of the stock. For example, if a stock's price is $100 per share and the annual dividend is $4 per share, the dividend yield is 4 percent. You can find the yields listed in the stock tables of *The Wall Street Journal*, so your math requirements are at a minimum if you choose to follow this investing strategy. Just follow these five steps:

1. List the 30 stocks of the DJIA on a sheet of paper.

2. Write down the current share price of each of these stocks next to its symbol.

3. Write down the yield for each stock next to its price.

4. Highlight the ten stocks with the highest yield.

5. Put a check next to the five lowest-priced stocks of the ten highest-yielding stocks that you've selected in the previous step.

O'Higgins suggests three options for selecting your portfolio on the basis of the chart you've just created:

1. Purchase equal amounts (in dollars) of all ten of the highest-yielding Dow stocks.

2. Purchase equal amounts (in dollars) of the five lowest-priced of the ten highest-yielding stocks.

3. Purchase only the second lowest-priced stock from among the ten highest-yielding stocks (the Penultimate Profit Prospect, or PPP, as O'Higgins calls it).

Your only maintenance requirement for any of these three portfolios is that exactly one year after you make your first investment, you reevaluate the stocks you purchased on the same yield-based and price-based criteria. If the stocks in your portfolio no longer match the selection criteria, sell those stocks and buy the new group of low-priced, high-yield Dow stocks. This evaluation is all you have to do to maintain a winning portfolio of stocks that has historically outperformed the Dow Jones Average year after year. For 15 minutes of effort per year, you can create an investment that can provide 20 percent or more returns on average.

O'Higgins points out that the risks in choosing the first portfolio of ten stocks are less than those of purchasing either of the smaller portfolios because of the greater degree of diversification you have. However, he also says that by buying the second portfolio (the five lowest-priced, high-yield Dow stocks), you significantly increase your chances of experiencing a greater profit than by buying all ten high-yielding stocks. By decreasing your risk, you tend to decrease the potential amount of your return. Investing in all ten of the highest yielding stocks may turn out to be somewhat safer, but because you have less risk, your possibilities for excellent returns are somewhat diminished. Finally, O'Higgins' research indicates that by purchasing the second lowest-

priced Dow stock from among the ten highest yielding stocks, you have the greatest chance of making the best profits, although by purchasing only one stock you significantly increase your risk—if this stock doesn't perform well, you aren't diversified at all and will suffer a loss.

Why does this strategy work? There are two reasons:

1. Investors all too often think in terms of the short term.

2. The DJIA stocks are among the strongest and most resilient companies in America, so investing in them is likely to be very safe and profitable as well.

NEW YORK ISN'T THE OLDEST

While New York City and the NYSE hold many fine distinctions that set them apart from other cities and exchanges, the fact is that the NYSE isn't the oldest stock exchange of the 138 exchanges listed throughout the world. The oldest stock exchange is the Amsterdam exchange in the Netherlands, which was founded in 1602.

This method exploits the fact that investors frequently get caught up in short-term thinking. All too often in the stock market, a company, no matter how strong, will experience a drop in share price if even the most insignificant bad news is announced. The highest yielding stocks are those that the market currently treats as out of favor. You know this because most companies, unless they're in real trouble, don't reduce the amount of their annual dividend. If the yield is high (the ratio of the dividend versus the price per share), it tells you that the market has placed a low value on the shares of that company. But because the Dow stocks are generally so strong and able to bounce back from setbacks, these temporarily out-of-favor stocks are very likely to return to their previous values, even surpass those values over time. This technique takes advantage of short-term fluctuations in the value of some of the best companies in the world.

The Foolish Four

A variation on *Beating the Dow,* the Foolish Four method combines the two riskier (and more profitable) options offered by O'Higgins into a single, extremely successful portfolio model. David and Tom Gardner offer this proposal in their excellent (and fun) book, *The Motley Fool Investment Guide*. Basically, the Fools' proposition combines the five highest-yielding, lowest-priced Dow stocks with the second lowest-priced of the highest-yielding stocks (the PPP stock). If the PPP stock by itself historically provides the best returns of all the Dow stocks, and buying the five highest-yielding and lowest-priced Dow stocks helps provide a certain amount of diversification, which would not be possible from buying just one stock, why not merge the methods? This combination has provided superior returns of over 25 percent per year, based on historical data over the past 20 years.

Instead of buying the five lowest-priced high-yielding Dow stocks as O'Higgins suggests, the Fools replace the very lowest-priced of these five stocks with additional shares of the PPP stock. Their research indicates that the lowest-priced of these five stocks has historically been a company that has been in genuine trouble, and if you eliminate this stock and replace it with more shares of the second lowest-priced stock (the PPP), your returns will be increased significantly. Instead of buying equal dollar amounts of the five stocks recommended by the original five-stock method, you would buy only four stocks and double up on the PPP stock. For example, if you had $5,000 to invest, using O'Higgins' five-stock rule, you'd buy $1,000 each of five stocks. If you use the Foolish Four method, you buy $2,000 of the PPP stock, and $1,000 each of the three remaining stocks. The Foolish Four process offers a certain degree of diversification along with superior returns over time.

There's No Such Thing as a Sure Thing

While all these methods have been proven by testing their results over many years, you must remember that these results are historical results. In other words, just because a particular method has yielded extraordinary returns over the past 20 or 30 years, the method is not guaranteed to provide such spectacular results in the future. However, the strategies presented here will give you a solid beginning to the process of selecting stocks for your own portfolio. If you follow these plans carefully and keep an eye on the performance of your investments over time, you're very likely to be able to outperform the market averages and reap excellent returns on your investments. But don't forget to keep studying and learning as much as possible about the companies in which you invest as well as the various investment methods. Knowledge is definitely power in the world of stocks. The more you know, the more your investments will grow.

MORE money- making ideas with STOCKS

CHAPTER SEVEN

Making money and buying and selling good quality stocks seems like a fairly simple proposition, once you've learned the basics and understand how the markets work. But you can make money in the **stock market** *in many other ways, and some of them don't require you to buy any stocks at all.*

Over the years, financial professionals have devised numerous variations on the basic theme of buying and selling stocks. For example, index funds are mutual funds that create portfolios based on the stocks in specific indexes. One of the most widely known index funds, as well as one of the first funds to use the methodology of reflecting the indexes, is the Vanguard 500 Index. The goal of the fund is to reflect the performance of the S&P 500 index by purchasing each and every stock in the index. Because roughly 75 percent of all mutual funds fail to perform better than the S&P

500, Vanguard's idea to create this investment vehicle is truly ingenious. Mutual funds, however, are one of the more simple variations on stock investing, and in this chapter we'll examine some of the more interesting options (pun intended) available to you as an investor.

Derivatives

The term derivative refers to a general class of investments rather than a specific type of investment like stocks or bonds. Derivatives are investment vehicles that are derived from other types of investments. In other words, derivatives are one or two (or even more) levels removed from the base investment. So, for example, an investment vehicle that is derived from the performance of stocks (such as options or futures) is a derivative of stock investments.

Stocks represent shares of ownership in something tangible, such as a corporation. Bonds also represent something tangible in that they are promises of loan repayments, or IOUs, from a borrower, whether a company or government entity. Derivatives are hybrid investments that are based on these more basic investments. Because they are hybrids, investing in derivatives is more complex, and often far more risky, than investing directly in stocks or bonds.

Two primary forms of derivatives are options and futures. These derivative investments can be based on stocks, bonds, precious metals, commodities such as corn or pork bellies, real estate, interest rates, market indexes, currencies and exchange rates, and many other investment types. While options and futures are complex and volatile investments, numerous other, even more complex derivatives exist in the financial markets, most of them not used by individual investors. Derivatives can become so complicated that even financial professionals have a hard time explaining them. While derivatives can be based on all sorts of investments, this chapter will focus on stock derivatives so you can see how they relate to the stock market and to your stocks in particular.

Options

An option is literally what its name indicates: if you own one, you have the option to buy or sell a block of 100 shares of a particular stock at a particular price, within a particular time frame. You don't actually own the stock, nor do you ever have to buy the stock to profit or lose money on options. But while options give you the right to buy or sell a stock as described, most investors never actually exercise their options by buying or selling the underlying stock. Because options have become investments in themselves, you can buy and sell them without ever putting your hands on any stocks at all. While options can be extremely volatile and risky investments, they can also serve the purpose of providing a hedge to protect investors from losses in particular stocks.

There are two types of options: puts and calls. A put option gives you the right to sell 100 shares of a specific stock at a given price, whereas a call option gives you the right to buy 100 shares of a stock in the same manner, all within a finite, predetermined period of time. Again, you don't actually ever have to buy or sell the stock; you can simply resell your options in the open market or let them expire if the set price isn't reached by the expiration date. Typically, you would buy call options if you expect the price of the underlying stock to rise, and you'd buy put options if you expect the price of the stock to decline. By purchasing a call option, or the right to buy a stock at a specified price within a set time frame, you would profit if the stock actually went up. You'd be able to buy the stock for a price that's less than the current market price of the stock, and then you could resell that stock immediately for a profit. For example, if you think IBM is going to go up in price, you could buy 100 shares now at $100 (for a total cost of $10,000). This purchase leaves you owning the shares and hoping they go up. Or you could buy one call option (representing 100 shares) at $2 per share, with a set price of $100 (for a total cost of $10,200). Here, you have the choice of exercising the option and buying the stock, and if it rises, you'll make a profit. If the stock doesn't rise in the time frame specified, you can let the option run out and take the $200 loss as a lesson learned, or you can sell the option to someone else and get some of your money back.

When you buy an option, you are buying a right that is sold on the open market by another party, whether an individual or a brokerage firm. The seller sets the expiration date and the strike price of the option. The strike price is the price at which you can actually exercise your option, if it is reached before the expiration date. So if on January 1 you bought ten call options for Goober's Mufflers (GOOB) with a strike price of $15 and an expiration date of March (options always expire on the third Friday of the specified month), and the current share price of GOOB is $8 per share, you're

expecting the price of GOOB to rise beyond $15 by the third week of March. If GOOB goes to $20 by the third week of March, you can exercise your option to buy 1,000 shares at $15, then immediately sell them back into the market for $20, thereby making a $5 per share profit. When you buy calls, your hope is that the actual price of the underlying stock will exceed your strike price before the expiration date of your options. The more the stock's price surpasses the strike price, the more money you can make.

Put options work in just the opposite way. Suppose you expect GOOB to drop like a rock between now and the end of March. You might then buy ten put options with a strike price of $5. If GOOB drops to $2 per share by the expiration date, you can exercise your option to sell 1,000 shares of GOOB stock at $5 per share. How can you sell this stock if you don't actually own any of it? Options themselves are tradable investments—an investor who bought shares of GOOB at $5 might be very interested in buying your options in order to sell the stock and break even instead of losing money.

Once an Option Is in the Money, Its Value Increases Tremendously

For both put and call options, if the underlying stock reaches the strike price before the expiration date, that option is said to be *at the money,* in which case the option really isn't worth all that much because it offers no advantage; anyone can buy the stock at the current market price. But if the price of the stock goes higher than the strike price, the option is said to be in the money if it is a call option, meaning that it can be exercised for a profit because you can buy the stock for less than the current market price. Conversely, a put option is *in the money* if the current stock price is less than the strike price of the option, because then you'd be able to sell the stock for more than the market price.

Any option that is in the money is going to be worth much more than an option that is at the money or *out of the money.* Out of the money options are those whose underlying stocks are below the strike price (for calls), or above the strike price (for puts). If you have the right or option to sell a stock at a specific price, you want the current market price to be less than that price, and the less the better so you can make a greater profit because of the difference. If you have five apples and the current price of an apple is 10 cents, but you've got a signed contract from your neighbor that says he'll buy those apples for 30 cents, you're clearly going to make a profit. On the other hand, if you've got the option to buy a stock at a specific price, you want that stock to sky-rocket to higher levels because then you'd be able to buy the stock at a great discount. So if apples currently cost 30 cents, but your neighbor has agreed to sell you some at a dime apiece, you're in pretty good shape.

Pricing Options and Risk

The price of options (called the premium), like the price of stocks, is in large part de-termined by market demand, but option prices are also influenced by the amount of time remaining before the expiration date of that option. So in addition to the intrin-sic value of an option, which is determined by the price of the underlying stock, you need to consider the time value of those options. The intrinsic value of an option is ac-tually a bit easier to figure than the intrinsic value of a stock, because the value of an option isn't necessarily tied to the valuation of the company itself but is directly tied to the price of the stock. You can determine the stock's price by checking the stock quotes in the newspaper or online or by consulting your broker.

So if you have a put option to sell a stock at $10, and the stock is currently trading at $8, the intrinsic value of the option is $2, the difference between the stock's price and your strike price. However, if your option is at the money or out of the money, that option has no intrinsic value because owning it brings no current advantage. If you have a put option with a strike price of $8, and the underlying stock's price is $8, the owner of the option doesn't have any advantage over anyone else who may want to buy the stock.

Why would anyone buy an option that's out of the money? Because the second con-sideration in pricing options is the time value of that option. Time value means the market acknowledges the fact that although the option isn't presently in the money, the price of the underlying stock may change before the expiration date and cause the option to be in the money. If you buy those put options with a strike price of $10, but the stock is currently trading at $12, you're likely to be able to get those options for less money than options that are in the money. You really have to believe that the stock's price is going to drop significantly before the expiration date if you decide you

Are You Risk-Tolerant or Risk-Averse?

Any investment involves a certain amount of risk, whether it be market risk, interest rate risk, or some other form of risk. But is all risk bad? The higher the risk you're willing to take, the higher the potential reward you could reap. Unfortunately, higher risk also implies a greater possibility of loss. It's like asking, "Is your glass half full or half empty?"

If you're the kind of investor who can stomach the inevitable downturns in the market because you realize that historically the stock market has been the best place to invest your money in the long run, you're probably a risk-tolerant investor. But if you are risk-averse, you're more likely to be afraid of bear markets and downswings, and if you get caught in one, you may find yourself selling all your stocks at a great loss.

One of the greatest assets an investor can have is self-knowledge. If you know you can't stand the thought of losing a single penny, you may be better off in a safer investment like a money market fund or bond fund, even though your returns will probably be lower in the long term than if you invested in stocks. You also need to have a clear picture of your own financial situation. If you can't afford to lose any money, make sure to choose more conservative investments.

want to take the risk and buy these options. But if the price of the stock does drop, you stand to make a pretty healthy profit. The rule of thumb is that the more time remaining before the expiration date, the greater the time value of the option, because the price of the stock may be able to change more over a long period of time than over a short period of time. If you buy five $1 puts that expire in one month on a stock now at $20 per share, the odds are against you. But if you have six months before expiration, many more things can happen to affect that stock adversely over six months than over a single month.

The risk of buying an option is easy to determine. Like stocks, the most you can lose if you buy an option is the price of admission. So if you buy those $10 puts at a premium of $2 per option, but the stock price never drops below $12 per share, you simply let the options expire and you lose the money you paid for those options—$2 apiece. The nice thing about buying options is that you always know the maximum downside if you lose your bet. But the upside of options is theoretically infinite, because it is only limited by the maximum price the stock can reach, which is also theoretically infinite. Suppose you bought $10 call options on a stock the current price of which is $5 per share. You will probably be able to get those options rather inexpensively because they're out of the money, although you need to remember that if there is a long time remaining before the options expire, the time value may increase the premium you'll pay. Then if that stock's price rises to, say, $100 before the expiration date, you'll have made quite a bundle.

Hedging

In addition to buying options for the speculative possibilities they afford, many investors buy them as a means of hedging their investments in actual stock. Investors use hedging to reduce the risks involved in their investments. If you bought 100 shares of GOOB at $10 per share six months ago, and today those shares are worth $16 per share, you could sell the shares and make a nice 60 percent profit—an enviable gain by anyone's standards. However, you may still feel optimistic that GOOB's price will continue to rise far beyond the current $16. In order to protect your gains, you might consider buying a put option with a strike price of $16 per share. That way, if GOOB actually drops back to $10 before the expiration date of your option, you can exercise the option to ensure that you haven't lost your gain.

Suppose the cost of the option was $50. If GOOB rises and you let your option expire, you've lost the money you used to buy the option, but you've still made plenty of money on the increase in GOOB's value. But if the stock drops back to $10, you can exercise your option to sell GOOB at $16, so your net profit will be $550, calculated as follows:

The selling price of the shares:	**$1,600**
Minus your purchase price:	− 1,000
Minus the option premium:	− 50
Equals your profit:	$ 550

In this case, you can easily see how great the hedging value of buying options can be. You can use options to protect your investments from potential losses over time, and the costs can be relatively little compared to the value you can get from this hedge.

Selling or Writing Options

When you buy options on the open market and decide to sell them back to make a profit, what you are doing is called closing your option position. You can also exercise your options by buying or selling the underlying stock, or you can let your options expire. But where do the options come from in the first place? Someone has to create those options so that other investors can buy them. This process is called writing or selling options.

There are two ways to write options: you can write covered options or naked options. The difference is critical and may make an enormous difference in the amount of risk you have to be willing to absorb by writing the options.

A covered option is written or sold by someone who actually owns the shares of the underlying stock. For example, if you own 1,000 shares of a stock at $25 per share, you can write ten call options with a strike price of $35 per share and collect the premium paid by the buyer of those options, say $500. If those options expire and the strike price is never reached, you've made a profit of $500 because the buyer couldn't exercise the option. But if the strike price is reached before the expiration date, you can either sell your stock to the buyer (if the option is exercised), or you can buy ten similar calls to offset the ones you wrote and keep the stock. In this case, you'll break even on the options because your cost of buying the calls will offset the premium you received from writing them.

But if you write a naked call option, you're taking a greater risk because you are writing options on stock that you don't own. Suppose you wrote those same $35 calls on that $25 stock, but you didn't actually own the underlying stock. If the strike price is reached and the buyer of the options decides to exercise them, you'll have to buy the 1,000 shares of stock at $35. That means it will cost you $35,000 to cover those options for a total loss of $34,500! If you ever decide to write naked options, you'll need to have quite a bit of confidence that the strike price will never be reached by the expiration date because, as you can see, your risk of loss is quite significant.

Most investors buy options rather than write them. Typically, institutional investors like mutual funds or very wealthy investors will write options to hedge other stock positions or simply to profit from the premiums, but individual investors aren't generally willing to take the risks involved with writing options. However, if you are interested in speculating and are willing to lose the entire amount of your investment, investing in options can be a way of making significant profits for relatively small cost. Options may also provide a good means of protecting any profits you make from your stock investments by offering a hedge against potential losses. While you can potentially lose your entire investment when you buy stocks, you aren't likely to experience that degree of loss if the company is a profitable and growing enterprise. But with options, you have a very limited window of time in which you want the price of the underlying stock to move in a certain direction. If those options expire, you are guaranteed to lose the entire premium you paid for them. But the upside of option investing can be phenomenal, if you're willing to take the risk.

Futures

Another form of derivative investment, futures or futures contracts, is an agreement to take delivery of a specific type of commodity at a particular price at some time in the future. The history of futures goes back to a day when agriculture was the primary industry in this country. Farmers and market speculators would agree on a specific price for a commodity, such as corn, that would be delivered at some future date. The future ensured that the farmer would get a good price for the crop when harvest time

Technical Analysis: Fact or Fiction?

Technical analysis is a tool used by market timers to determine appropriate times to buy and sell stock. While technical analysis theories have a great number of adherents, most of the very successful investors like Warren Buffett and Peter Lynch tend to invest on the basis of value, or the fundamentals, of a company rather than on obscure trends in the stock's price. They feel that the price of a stock over the past month has very little to do with the price of that stock in the upcoming month.

As you invest more and more, you'll see the standard disclaimer, particularly when you're looking at mutual funds, that says: "Past performance is no guarantee of future returns." Engrave that little phrase into the palm of your hand so that whenever you decide to pick up the phone and order stock based on the patterns in a chart, you'll ask yourself again whether that's really the wisest course of action.

Technical analysts talk about resistance, a theoretical upper limit that appears to stop the price of a stock from rising further, and support, which is a sort of bottom level price below which a stock can't seem to drop. While these patterns may have some psychological basis, in that investors may have somehow collectively decided that the stock really isn't worth more or less than certain dollar amounts, the fact is that any stock can go higher or lower than these imagined resistance or support levels. As Peter Lynch might say: Invest in good companies, and your stocks will take care of themselves.

came, even if the market price of corn had dropped in the meantime. The speculators who were on the other end of these contracts would hope that the market price for corn would increase so they could take delivery of the commodity and then resell it at a higher price. Manufacturers would also enter into futures contracts to protect themselves from the risk of higher prices on commodities. A cereal maker might buy futures to guarantee that it could buy corn at a specific price in the future, even if the market price rose in the meantime.

These days, futures have become investments in their own right, and they're bought and sold just like stocks or options. Although originally the underlying assets for futures were commodities, now the underlying assets can be currency exchange rates, precious metals, and such intangibles as stock market indexes. Because futures imply the delivery of a specific commodity or asset at some time in the future, however, how can futures be traded on indexes, which can't be delivered to anyone? Index futures are based on speculation regarding the general direction of the market, not on anything that can be physically exchanged like a commodity. So the deliverable, in the case of index futures, is cash. The way index futures are priced is by taking the index number and multiplying it by $250. So if the S&P 500 index is currently in the 1,500 range, the price of an S&P 500 index futures contract would be $375,000 (1,500 × $250), which leaves out most beginning investors.

Individual investors rarely take advantage of these type of investments, in large part because of the high prices involved. However, institutional investors use index futures to hedge against market movements that could negatively impact their funds. Although a mutual fund manager in charge of a portfolio that's similar in composition to the S&P 500 can buy and sell stocks to try to keep the fund profitable, preventing losses may be impossible if there's a general market downturn, when nearly all stocks are dropping in price. If the S&P 500 index is at 100, to hedge against the possibility of a market downturn, the manager might sell a futures contract to a speculator (who expects the market to rise rather than fall) that specifies a future index value of 110. The speculator expects the index to rise, and if it does the fund manager can get out of the futures market by buying another contract to offset the losses on this one. But if the market falls and the index reaches 90, the fund manager can sell the contract at a profit, thereby offsetting the losses of the underlying stocks in the mutual fund portfolio.

Options on futures contracts give you the right to buy or sell a specific futures contract for a specific price if the strike price of the option is reached before the expiration date. In other words, this kind of investment gives you the option to buy or sell an agreement to buy or sell something. Imagine how complex your own portfolio could become if you dabbled in this type of derivative investment. Nonetheless, a tremendous market exists for these investments because plenty of money can be made, and plenty of speculators and hedgers are willing to engage in these investment vehicles. Remember, as is the case with stocks or any other investment: The higher the risk you're willing to take, the greater the possible reward you may gain.

Shorting Stock

This method of investing involves making a profit on stocks not if they increase in value, but if they decrease in value. How can you make money on a stock if the value drops? As you've seen already, making money on declining stock values is possible if you purchase options. For example, if you thought a stock was overpriced and about to decline, you could buy put options that would give you the right to sell the stock at a certain price, hopefully higher than the market price of the stock, before the expiration date of the option. Shorting stock is similar in that you're betting that the stock price will decline. However, when you short a stock, you don't have to worry about an expiration date as you do with options. Here's how it works.

Selling short is like a credit arrangement with your broker. When you call your broker and request that you want to "short 100 shares of GOOB," your broker borrows the shares from another investor, then sells those shares immediately on the open market and deposits the proceeds into your account. Most brokers require that you be approved and have at least some money, usually at least 50 percent of the value of the transaction, in your margin account before they'll let you short stocks. While your account may look like you scored big just by asking to short a stock, the fact is that you haven't yet made any money because you're living on borrowed funds.

For you to profit on a short sale, the price of the stock must drop below the price of the stock at the time you placed your short trade. Then you call your broker and tell him to close your short position. The broker buys the same number of shares that you shorted and returns them to the lender. Because you bought the shares at a lower price

than the price of the shares at the time you borrowed them, you get to keep the difference in cash.

For example, suppose GOOB is trading at $10 per share. You think this baby is going to drop like a hot potato, so you get excited, call your broker, and say, "Short me 1,000 shares of that GOOB stock!" Your broker goes through the necessary gyrations and will shortly deposit $10,000 into your account (1,000 × $10 = $10,000). Your luck is good this month, and within the next few weeks GOOB stock has dropped to a measly $5 per share. Realizing that a 50 percent profit is pretty amazing for only a few weeks' work, you contact your broker to place an order to close your short position. The broker buys 1,000 shares of GOOB at $5, returns the shares to the original (and by now quite unhappy) owner, and you're left sitting on a pile of cash worth $5,000. What's the risk if the stock's price rises? Theoretically, you have what is known as unlimited upside risk when you short a stock. This means that if the stock climbs forever and you never close your short position, you'll wind up broke, bankrupt, and probably very bummed out. Consider again the previous example. If you short 1,000 shares of GOOB at $10, and the stock price climbs to $20, you're looking at a $20,000 dollar loss. How can that be if you never actually bought the shares to begin with? If you decide to close your position at $20, you'll have to buy 1,000 shares of GOOB at $20, and shell out $20,000 just to repay the person who loaned you the stock in the first place, which can be worse than buying GOOB at $10 and watching it drop to nothing. Your risk with buying a stock is limited to the amount you invested in it. But your risk with shorting is, theoretically anyway, unlimited.

What are some strategies to make money by shorting? Consider the valuation of the company. Just as when you are investing by doing fundamental analysis to find underpriced companies, you can use the same techniques to try to find overpriced companies. Suppose GOOB has just gone through an amazing six-month runup in price because it was the latest hot stock on the street. If the company's growth rate is at 20 percent per year but the stock is trading at a PE of 100, you may have hit on a good short opportunity. Often the markets will drive the price of certain stocks to ridiculously high levels, only to let them drop back when people realize the stock isn't going to earn infinitely large sums of cash. These high-flying stocks may be just what the doctor ordered for someone who's interested in shorting. You should also set a specific limit to the amount of money you're willing to lose on a short investment. You may

want to commit yourself to closing your position if the stock's price increases 10 or 20 percent beyond the price when you shorted it. This way you'll prevent massive losses from a stock that climbs too high.

You have two good reasons to limit your losses when you short a stock. The first, somewhat unlikely scenario is that you may be forced by your broker to close your short position. If the person who loaned you the shares wants to get them back and your broker can't find anyone else willing to loan the shares, you may have to close your position sooner than you'd like. This situation is very rare, though it can occur, primarily with stocks that have a very small number of shares outstanding.

The second circumstance that could cause a short position to close is known as a short squeeze. This happens particularly in cases where many people are holding short positions in a stock. If the stock price rises to a level that makes a large number of shorts uncomfortable, they may all decide to cut their losses at once and close their positions. Their combined decisions cause a huge upswing in buying activity on the market, which drives up the stock price. Getting caught in a short squeeze is one of the most uncomfortable experiences a stock investor can ever have. You may sit helplessly watching the stock price rise through the stratosphere, while your broker clamors to buy back the borrowed shares as soon as possible. But if you're able to limit your losses by deciding in advance how much you can stand to lose, shorting stock may be a great complement to your overall investing strategy.

Buying on Margin

Buying stocks on margin isn't so much a strategy or a type of investment as it is a way of getting some additional funding to buy more stock. Most brokerage firms will offer their clients the ability to borrow a certain amount of money to purchase additional shares of stock, if they already have a certain amount of money in their accounts—usually at least 50 percent of the amount they want to borrow—in cash or in stock. So if you want to buy $10,000 worth of shares on margin, you'll need to have at least $5,000 in cash or stock in your account.

Buying stock on margin can be risky but is less so than shorting stocks, because the total downside is limited to the amount of money you borrowed. Nonetheless, it can

be more difficult psychologically to lose money you didn't even have to begin with than to lose money you already had; you'll have to scrounge up the cash to repay your broker if your investment doesn't live up to your expectations. If you aren't careful when you invest on margin, you could dig yourself a pretty big hole from which it may be difficult to climb.

Another consideration for buying on margin is the risk of what is known as a margin call. Because your broker has the right to expect not to lose the entire amount of your loan, you may be required to put additional cash or stock into your account if the securities you bought on margin decrease to a certain level. Or your broker may require additional cash if the total value of the equity in your account drops below a certain level.

A margin call is another of those unpleasant market realities, like a short squeeze, that can really hurt if you get caught in it. You may have had the best intentions in the world of repaying your margin loan by a certain date, but if the stock you bought on margin drops significantly in price, you will need to repay your broker or face some gnarly legal troubles.

THE GREAT DEPRESSION

People recall the date of October 29, 1929, as "Black Tuesday," the date of the infamous stock market crash that many believe began the Great Depression. But the overall Depression affected the stock markets far more deeply than the drop of that single day. On Black Tuesday, the Dow Jones Industrial Average, which had reached 381.71 on September 3, 1929, dropped 30.57 points. But the lowest point for the Dow after the crash didn't occur until July 2, 1932, when the average reached a bottom of 41.22 points.

Choose Your Weapons Wisely

Investment vehicles like options and futures and a strategy like shorting stocks can offer the lure of enormous returns with relatively little downside risk, but you need to weigh those risks very carefully in comparison to the amount of the potential rewards. While you know in advance, for example, that by buying options your total downside is limited to the entire amount of money you invested, you should be prepared for the

very real possibility that your options might expire worthless. If you can deal with the loss of $1,000 in three months to take the chance of making many more thousands if you guess right, for example, options may be an investment approach for you to consider. In the same way, shorting stocks can enable you to profit from stock you "just know" is going to decline in value. But as is the case with any investment, you never know in advance the direction the price is going to take. When you invest, make sure you understand the downside potential of your investment, and be clear and honest with yourself about how much money you can actually tolerate losing.

USING the Internet as a prime SOURCE

*Although this book doesn't require or assume that you're going to be **online**, these days a savvy investor cannot possibly ignore the subject of the Internet as one of the **best investment tools** available today.*

Although you don't need to be online to buy stocks, savvy investors know that the Internet is one of the best investment tools available today. While you could probably pursue profitable investments without it, the Internet offers resources that are unmatched by any single print source. If you're wired, you get instant access to literally thousands of investment services, publications, newsletters, and discussion groups from the comfort of your living room or office. You can buy a copy of *The Wall Street Journal* every morning at the newsstand, but you can't search the text of the paper for a specific company or keyword without flipping through page after page of irrelevant material. Nor can you pick up the *Journal,* then flip to *Investor's Business Daily, BusinessWeek, Time,* and *Newsweek* in the time it takes to click a button on your screen.

Print publications are not obsolete, however, and they are still valuable reference materials. But the Internet gives you the means to find more information from more places fast. Because of the incomparable speed and availability of data online, the world of the Internet should be foremost among your arsenal of research weapons.

Why is the Internet so exciting? One minute you're reading *The Wall Street Journal*, and then you click a button and you're perusing *Investor's Business Daily*. Click another button, and you can see a *Newsweek* article about a company you've been tracking. You can also use search engines like Yahoo! or Alta Vista. Just enter the name of the company you want to research, and within seconds you've got a thousand links to information in places ranging from *The Chicago Tribune* to the Securities and Exchange Commission's online database. If you haven't experienced the wonders of the Web, get yourself out there—you'll be amazed at what you can find.

This chapter isn't going to take you through the process of finding an Internet provider and getting you online—books are available that will do just that. This chapter will explore the world of the cyberspace stock market. The Internet is exploding with information on investments—so get connected and check it out.

Newsgroups and Useful Forums

One of the best ways to find information about good investments and services is to talk to other people who have been there before you. The Internet gives you the perfect means to contact thousands of investors around the world who are, like you, trying to be successful in the stock market. A good way to keep in touch with other investors is to participate in the Internet's Usenet newsgroups. While the name newsgroups makes it sound like you'll be chatting online with Walter Cronkite and Dan Rather, what actually happens is that people from different parts of the globe get to share information and news. Newsgroups are like an electronic bulletin board where individuals post messages that can be read and responded to by anyone who has access.

Thousands of newsgroups are on the Internet, and they cover topics ranging from medicine and sports to computers and investments. The investment topics can be broad in scope, talking about all types of investments, or quite narrow, with a specialized focus such as options or futures.

To participate in newsgroups, you need to have an Internet connection and specialized software, either a newsreader or an Internet browser that has Usenet capabilities. The two most widely used Internet browsers are Netscape Navigator and Microsoft Internet Explorer. If you belong to an online service like America Online or CompuServe, you'll either have access to a proprietary browser offered by that service, or you'll be able to get one of the other two browsers.

One of the most popular and active newsgroups for stock market investors can be found at misc. invest.stocks. This group is dedicated, as its name would suggest, to wide-ranging discussions about stocks and the stock market. You'll be able to share information with other investors who are interested in all aspects of the stock market, from value investing to technical analysis.

Discussions about hot stocks or losers are also common here, and you'll be able to touch base with investors who have had experiences similar to yours. Interesting discussion threads have included such topics as "bonehead moves of 1996," in which participating individuals shared stories of their investing mistakes for the year. (They talked of buying too high, selling too soon, listening to their brokers instead of their hearts, and other sad tales.) Also, "the coming crash" was mentioned, and people predicted the end of the bull market—"the market's way too high, gotta come down soon!" You can also start your own discussions if you're interested in particular subjects or individual stocks.

PEARLS OF WISDOM

"Never Fall in Love with a Stock."

Regardless of how much you may really like a company or a particular stock, don't make emotional attachments. Invest wisely in profitable and successful business ventures. If you bought a particular stock when it was a sad and lonely penny stock and you watched it increase in value to $20 per share, congratulations! You've succeeded in a way that most investors only wish for.

But don't let sentiment about the stock affect your decision to sell it if the company starts slipping. Many investors hold stocks while they climb rapidly, then watch in despair as the stock price starts sliding backward. Far too many people have looked back with sadness when they realized they let a nice profit dwindle away because they were too attached to a stock to sell it.

The range of discussions here is limited only by the general expectation that the topic will have something to do with stocks.

Other newsgroups cover topics like futures, options, mutual funds, and technical analysis:

- *misc.invest.canada* Investing in Canadian companies and markets.

- *misc.invest.commodities* Interested in pork bellies and orange juice? This is the newsgroup for you.

- *misc.invest.emerging* Find out about emerging opportunities and industries, growth stocks, and the next hot investment.

- *misc.invest.forex* Covers foreign exchange and currency markets.

- *misc.invest.mutual-funds* For mutual fund investors. Compare notes, complain about fees, all under one cyberroof.

- *misc.invest.futures* All about speculative investments.

- *misc.invest.index-futures* More speculation. Try to guess where the markets are heading and bet on those derivatives.

- *misc.invest.options* Information about puts and calls.

- *misc.invest.precious-metals* Gold, silver, and platinum.

- *misc.invest.real-estate* Share knowledge and experience about real estate investing.

- *misc.invest.stocks* The most popular group for stock investors. You can find information about almost any stock.

- *misc.invest.stocks.penny* If you're looking for information about penny stocks, you'll find it here. This isn't a terribly active group, but it has its focus.

- *misc.invest.technical* Do you like to analyze charts? Have you bought new trend analysis software? Discuss your technical theories here.

The World Wide Web for Investors

While newsgroups give you a good interactive way to discuss stocks with other investors, the World Wide Web is the best place to do research on stocks and find information about companies, including brokerage firms. Newsgroups are very active in terms of investor participation, and you'll be sure to get inundated with opinions from all kinds of people, but much of the information is unreliable or questionable at best because it is often based on nothing but opinion. You'll often run into messages that tout the next killer stock. Be very wary of these. More often than not, the proponent has something to gain by your investment.

If, however, you're trying to find more factual information, or if you want to contact a company directly, the Web is the place to do it. You do need to have your critical faculties wide awake when you're browsing on the Web. Sometimes a company will present information that is slanted or inaccurate because it wants to put its best foot forward and make a positive impression. But the Web gives you the means to find the details that can put things in proper perspective. If you visit a company's Web site and all you see is information about what an amazing return you'll get on your investment, you can surf right on over to *The Wall Street Journal* or *Investor's Business Daily* online site to see if they have any stories about that company.

You can also check in with government agencies like the Securities and Exchange Commission to verify data. Make sure you check your facts. Don't let yourself be led into an investment because one analyst or one article seems positive; always find out more. The World Wide Web gives you the means to do the kind of research that used to be the sole province of professional analysts and investment advisers. Take advantage of it, and make it work for your bottom line.

Fortunately, the opportunities presented by the Internet have spurred the creation of numerous Web sites dedicated to providing investors with unbiased and well-researched information. So in addition to being able to visit IBM's Web site to find out what the company has been up to and to read the balance sheet and annual report, you can jump over to the Silicon Investor Web site to read a profile of the company and to see what other investors have to say about its future prospects. The number of Web sites created specifically for investors has increased significantly in the past few years, so you won't have any problem finding good, solid information to help you make your investment decisions.

Researching Stocks and Brokers on the Net

Finding company Web sites on the Internet is usually a fairly straightforward process. Most Web addresses (also known as URLs) follow the same format as the Microsoft home page, for example. This address is < www.microsoft.com >. To find other company home pages, you can try replacing the Microsoft part of this address with the name of the company you're looking for. For instance, the IBM address is < www.ibm.com > and the Netscape Web site is < www.netscape.com >. Sometimes the address uses the company's initials, as in the Merrill Lynch address < www.ml.com > or the Morgan Stanley Dean Witter address < www.msdw.com >.

If you're having trouble finding a company's site, you can use a search engine on the Internet such as Alta Vista < www.altavista.com > or Google < www.google.com > to find company Web sites. (You can also call the company and ask what their Internet address is.) Most of these sites have special areas dedicated to providing information to investors, so these places would be great starting points when you're researching companies.

In addition to finding information about specific companies, you can also find brokerage and mutual fund firms on the Web. When you visit a brokerage service online, you can find out about their services, request a prospectus for particular investments, learn about the fees they charge, and find out whether they offer online investment and trading capabilities. If you're a wired investor and are interested in doing most of your investment research and trading online, you should visit some of these brokerage firms on the Web. Most of the brokerages and mutual fund companies that have a Web presence offer online stock or fund quotes, and some of the full-service firms provide research information on the Web to their customers. You may also discover that some sites have regular columns and articles about investing strategies that can help you in your continuing stock education.

Here are the Web addresses of some brokerages and mutual fund firms:

- Ameritrade < www.ameritrade.com >

- E*TRADE < www.etrade.com >

- Datek < www.datek.com >

- Discover Brokerage <www.discoverbrokerage.com>

- DLJ Direct <www.dljdirect.com>

- Fidelity Investments <www.fidelity.com>

- Goldman Sachs <www.gs.com>

- Lebenthal <www.lebenthal.com>

- Legg Mason <www.leggmason.com>

- Merrill Lynch <www.mldirect.ml.com>

- Morgan Stanley Dean Witter <www.msdw.com>

- Salomon Smith Barney <www.smithbarney.com>

- Charles Schwab <www.schwab.com>

- TD Waterhouse <www.tdwaterhouse.com>

This list is by no means exhaustive but is rather a small subset of the possibilities available on the Web. If you visit a few of these sites, you'll begin to get an idea of just how much quality information is available out there for investors. If you want to find the site of a company not listed here, consult one of the search engines on the Net, and you'll be connected in a wink.

Do you want an unbiased opinion about a particular broker, service, or mutual fund? Visit the Usenet newsgroups to find investors who will be more than happy to share their knowledge. One of the best ways to find information about services is to ask people who have used them. If someone has had a bad experience with a particular brokerage or service, you can bet your life that they'll be eager to share that information with you. And the same goes for people who have been satisfied with the services they've received. You can even start an online poll to get people's opinions about companies you're considering if you haven't seen any messages relating to topics you're interested in.

Some Web sites are dedicated solely to providing information to investors. These sites are usually not affiliated with particular brokerage or mutual fund firms, so you're

more likely to get a good overview of the services available without feeling a sense that you're being sold on a particular service. In some ways, the Internet is a huge advertising and public relations medium. The companies want your business, and they aren't going to emphasize their flaws. You can bet that they'll try to give you the rosiest picture of their services. So if you find good, third-party investment sites that aren't financed by or affiliated with specific firms, you can count on a clear, unprejudiced analysis of the benefits of one company over another. Because these sites exist solely for the benefit of investors, you'll also be able to find information about specific stocks and mutual funds. Some Web sites even have their own discussion areas (similar to newsgroups), where you can talk about stocks and brokerage firms with other investors.

Here are a few of the investment-oriented Web sites:

- Barron's Online <www.barrons.com>

- Bloomberg <www.bloomberg.com>

- BusinessWeek <www.businessweek.com>

- CNET Investor <www.cnet.com>

- Edgar Online <www.edgar-online.com>

- Financial Web <www.stocktools.com>

- Hoover's Online <www.hoovers.com>

- IPO.com <www.ipo.com>

- Morningstar <www.morningstar.com>

- Quote.com <www.quote.com>

- Raging Bull <www.ragingbull.com>

- Silicon Investor <www.siliconinvestor.com>

- Smart Money <www.smartmoney.com>

- Stock Point <www.stockpoint.com>

- The Motley Fool <www.fool.com>

- TheStreet.com <www.thestreet.com>

- Validea.com <www.validea.com>

- Wall Street Journal Interactive
  <www.wsj.com>

In addition to the commercial and privately run investment sites on the Web, you can also find government agencies such as the SEC and the IRS online. These resources are great when you are trying to find earnings reports for companies (available by using the SEC's Edgar archives on the Web) or if you have tax-related questions about your capital gains or losses. (The IRS Web site is actually quite helpful.) You can also visit the Web sites of all the major exchanges including the NYSE, Nasdaq, and AMEX markets. These sites provide tons of historical information about the markets, and they also offer comprehensive listings of the companies that are traded on those exchanges as well as profiles and information about those companies. A good place to find Web addresses for exchanges and stock markets worldwide is the Rutgers University Stock and Commodity Exchanges index at <www.libraries.rutgers.edu/rul/index>.

Here are the addresses of some specific sites, including URLs for a few international exchanges:

- American Stock Exchange <www.amex.com>

- Chicago Board of Trade <www.cbot.com>

PEARLS OF WISDOM

"Trying to Catch a Falling Stock Is Like Trying to Catch a Falling Knife."

William O'Neil's C-A-N S-L-I-M method for picking stocks portrays this aphorism well. A stock that is rising in value is quite likely to keep rising for some time (if the fundamentals of the company are strong), while a stock that's dropping in price is just as likely to keep falling. Don't try to reach for a stock that's dropping rapidly in price just because it may have recently reached a 52-week low or because it looks like a bargain. The reasons behind a stock's drop in value may not be directly evident to you, but the market is clearly indicating that something's wrong. If the stock is on a downward trend and you're still interested in it, watch its pace for a few days or weeks to see how it goes before you jump into the ring.

- Chicago Mercantile Exchange <www.cme.com>

- Chicago Stock Exchange <www.chicagostockex.com>

- FTSE International <www.ftse.com>

- Internal Revenue Service <www.irs.ustreas.gov>

- London Stock Exchange AIM (Alternative Investment Market) <www.stockex.co.uk/aim>

- Nasdaq Stock Market <www.nasdaq.com>

- New York Mercantile Exchange <www.nymex.com>

- New York Stock Exchange <www.nyse.com>

- Philadelphia Stock Exchange <www.phlx.com>

- Securities and Exchange Commission <www.sec.gov>

Buying and Selling Stocks on the Net

When you've completed your research and made your decisions about the stocks you want to buy and/or sell, it's time to contact your broker and place those trades. If you're online, you don't even have to disconnect your modem to call your broker to place your orders. Have no fear, Internet commerce is here. If you've got an account with a brokerage firm that offers online trading service, you can go to their Web site, enter your account number and a personal identification number for security, and look at your account information right there on your Web browser. Click another button or a hot-link on your broker's Web page, and you'll go to an online order form. Just enter the stocks you want to buy, fill in the appropriate information, click another button, and you've placed your order. Now you can surf right back over to *The Wall Street Journal* and catch up on the latest news, without skipping a beat or logging off your computer.

If you've already got an account with a brokerage firm, you should either visit their Web site or call on the phone to find out if they offer online trading services. Many discount brokers offer Internet trading, and more and more of the bigger brokerage firms are getting into the game. Eventually, they'll quite likely all be offering online trading services because of the cost benefits to customers and because the demand for these services is growing every day. And if you call your broker after reading this and they tell you that they aren't on the Web yet, you can bet your life that they'll give serious consideration to getting online when you mention that you're taking your business to a competitor with online trading capabilities.

Here are some of the best sites that trade stocks on the Internet, according to e-commerce authority gomez.com:

- Charles Schwab <www.schwab.com>

- E*TRADE <www.etrade.com>

- Fidelity Investments <www.fidelity.com>

- DLJ Direct <dljdirect.com>

- TD Waterhouse <tdwaterhouse.com>

The Internet offers an amazing array of resources that cannot be found in any other single place. And as the number of people using the Internet continues to grow, more and more companies will find the reasons increasingly compelling to make their services available. Experts speculate that the Internet will become the largest single medium of commercial activity over the next few years, so you'd be wise to get online now and start exploring—a great resource is the *Online Trading Survival Guide* (Dearborn Trade, 2000). There's no telling what exciting and useful information you'll find as you begin to delve into the wonders of the World Wide Web.

IT'S *art,* intuition, *and* SCIENCE

CHAPTER NINE

*Is investing an **art** or is it a **science**? In the interest of providing a broad-based overview of the process of investing, this chapter will present a few philosophical ruminations on stocks and **stock pickings.***

We'll let you decide. This chapter will give you some food for thought as you place your trades. You can ponder these deep thoughts while you're on hold with your brokerage firm or as you watch the Quotron ticker tick away on your computer screen.

A Scientific Venture or an Adventure in Art?

The question of whether or not investing in stocks is a strictly scientific venture is one of the eternal debates that has plagued thoughtful investors for years. As long as people have been trading one thing or another for something else, they've been trying to

figure out how to maximize their returns. In the old days, if I had two sheep and I wanted three of your cows, you might not be willing to make a straight trade. Now if I threw in my first born or a string of beads, you might be more likely to sign the contract. The art of coercion has helped a number of people throughout history to get more of whatever they wanted, but generally speaking, you don't have this option in the stock market. You also have to consider the ethics behind your methods if you're at all honest about it. And if you aren't honest about it, you'll have to add imprisonment risk to the list of potential risks you'll face in your investing escapades.

In Chapter Six, you read about various techniques and strategies for investing that were designed by successful professional investors. These have been tested over time and, if you read more about these methods, you'll find that the creators have run the numbers back 10, 20, or 30 years to show that their systems are reliable, profitable, and safe. You also learned about value investing, which teaches you to buy stocks based on the fundamental strength of the underlying corporations, and you were introduced to technical analysis as a means of studying charts and graphs of stock performance to attempt to predict future price movements.

These methods all assume one thing in common: that investing is generally a predictable process that can be rationally understood and methodically quantified into strategies that can reliably produce profits. The underlying philosophy of these methods, whether or not they clearly state it, is that picking stocks is basically a science— something that can be analyzed and quantified and broken down into workable theories that can achieve results that can be reproduced.

So can you count on guaranteed profits if you follow a (fundamentally scientific) method that has proven itself over the past 30 years? Even the masters of the various investing techniques would probably hesitate to say that you can always expect profits if you follow their strategies to the letter. And no doubt they would all agree that even though a method shows impressive and consistent numbers over the past three decades, you can't be absolutely certain that you'll be able to repeat those numbers consistently in the future.

Does this mean that successful investing is a completely random and inexplicable skill that no one can define with any certainty? The answer is not a clear-cut yes or no, but rather a definite maybe. No matter how well a strategy or investment has performed in the past, there is no absolute certainty that it will continue to be useful and successful in the future. Nonetheless, selecting quality stocks is not a completely random activity because if you study the history of the markets and of successful stocks, you'll be able to pick out characteristics that are common to all stocks that have performed well. In fact, the technique of studying past performance is usually how strategies like C-A-N S-L-I-M and the Dow Dividend approach are created. As Peter Lynch says, "You can't always determine short-term price movements, but in the long run the stocks of good companies will always perform."

So yes, a certain amount of science or predictability is inherent in the process of investing. You can pretty much rest assured that a company that is losing money or losing customers or that is just plain mismanaged is not going to have a terribly successful stock. You can also generally expect that the stock of a profitable company is going to be a good investment, over the long term. But there have been plenty of cases of very strong companies that have had very mediocre stock performance and weak companies with strong stock performance. How can these anomalies be explained?

The stock market is affected by psychology and emotion as much as by any kind of predictable measure of a specific company's success. The markets are populated by people, and people react to all sorts of things in addition to the basic performance of a specific company. Rumors can affect a stock's price tremendously, sometimes for years, even if the rumors have no basis in fact. Also, many stocks are simply out of favor with investors for long periods of time. For whatever reason, some stocks will not perform exceedingly well no matter how strong the company behind the stock happens to be. The stock may be in an industry that hasn't caught the interest of investors, or it may be that the company handles its investor relations in such a way as to alienate investors. Picking the stocks that will perform seems to involve a certain amount of art in addition to science, in the sense that unpredictable factors can always affect investments, and these factors make the science part of the equation not consistently reliable.

Past Performance and Predicting the Future

The inherent uncertainty of all investments stems from the fact that you cannot absolutely accurately predict the future by using strictly scientific methods. For example, technical analysis relies on the recurrence of specific patterns of price movements to

The Miracle of Compounding

The basic gist of compounding is that as your initial investment earns interest, you begin to earn interest on that interest.

The frequency at which the interest rate is compounded has a strong effect on the amount of money you'll have earned by the end of the year. If your investment compounds annually, you only get extra money in your fund or account once a year. But if the interest is compounded daily, for example, you get a little bit more money added to your account each and every day.

The mathematical calculations used to figure compound interest are complex, but the way compounding works is like a snowball effect. The annual interest rate figure is divided by the period of compounding (12 for monthly, 365 for daily, and so on). Then the resulting figure is multiplied by the principal amount each period and added to the investment. So if the annual rate is quoted at 5 percent and the interest is compounded monthly, you figure the monthly rate as $.05 \div 12 = .004167$. If you had invested $1,000, you can calculate what you'll have after the first month like this: $1,000 \times 1.004167 = \$1,004.17$. Next month you do the same calculation with the new figure : $1,004.17 \times 1.004167 = \$1,008.35$.

If you draw this series of calculations out over a year, you'll see that if your 5 percent investment is compounded monthly, you'll have $1,051.16 instead of $1,050.00 (what you'd have if the interest were compounded annually) at the end of the year. You need to look for two important factors when considering investments that pay interest: the rate of interest and the frequency of compounding. Look for higher numbers in both categories, and you're well on your way to solid long-term returns.

determine future price movements. While certain patterns may repeat themselves and become apparent to chartists, a pattern that was seen in the past will not necessarily repeat itself in the future.

What does the pattern of a stock's chart over the past year have to do with the current market psychology or attitude about that stock anyway? Fundamental investors would answer, "Absolutely nothing." But technical analysis investors might say that the patterns reflect the psychology of the markets even better than does the analysis of the company's fundamentals, and therefore the charts can help determine how a stock's price is likely to react in the future more than an analysis of the company's balance sheet.

If the truth is that you cannot clearly determine how a stock's price will perform in the future, then how can some investors have consistently excellent investment performance year after year after year? Names that come to mind include Warren Buffett, George Soros, and Peter Lynch. While these legendary investors may not agree that much of their success comes from a certain knack for picking stocks, others would claim that the art of investing is at least as important as the science of it.

The art of investing includes the ability to make buy or sell decisions at appropriate times, as well as the aptitude for holding on to good stocks even during rough times. Some investors have the uncanny genius for being able to determine the right moment to sell a certain stock just before its fortunes turn for the worse or to buy a stock at the right time and hang on to it for terrific profits, and this skill is difficult, if not impossible, to quantify.

Considering all the conditions that made a stock successful in the past and determining if those conditions still apply is certainly part of the process of successful investing. Following the value method, for example, requires that you keep your eyes on a company's fundamentals. If you notice the fundamentals change for the worse, you might consider that a sign to sell your stock. If the company has one or two bad quarters, the fundamentals may look lousy for a couple of reporting periods, but this setback may be just temporary. If you strictly evaluated the past performance of the stock and compared it to current performance, you might be led to assume that the company is heading for bad times and sell your stock. But selling might turn out to be a mistake because the company may rebound after this short-term upset. You may have even sold

for a loss because you were worried that the stock would continue falling or because you've seen the fundamentals change from what they were in the past. Although the process of evaluating a company involves an understanding of that company's history and previous performance, you must remember that you can't drive a car while staring into the rearview mirror. You've got to be able to look ahead and try to make your decisions based on what is likely to happen in the future, no simple task by any means.

Intuition versus Reason

Numerous factors, both logical and illogical, affect the performance of a stock. The art of investing involves the ability to assimilate a great deal of information and interpret it correctly. Much of this process is done through the faculty of intuition rather than reason. Somehow, successful investors are able to determine that the two bad quarters are a fluke or a temporary recession on the road to recovery. They may even take advantage of this period to buy more stock at a lower price, because they sense in some inexplicable way that the stock is only going through a limited drop in value.

A fundamental investor might be tempted to think that the company's fortunes have turned and that the drop is the beginning of a negative period for the company, while a technical investor might consider the chart and interpret the downward movement as a sign to sell the stock. The process of developing intuition and that sixth sense that seems to be the province of so many successful people in diverse disciplines is well described in many books on the subject. One resource that is of particular interest to investors is Robert Koppel's *The Intuitive Trader.* Koppel is no stranger to the real world of investing, so his book carries the additional weight of having been written by a very successful trader who believes that intuition can be one of the best resources available to an investor.

In addition to the inscrutable mystery of intuition, however, you must learn the art of absorbing information from various sources and acting upon that information in such a way that your investments will be profitable. This skill probably comes more with practice over a period of time than through some mysterious and unknown talent, however. Just as an individual can develop a facility for playing a musical instrument if they devote enough time and energy to learning techniques and practicing them, so can anyone learn enough to be successful in the stock market. By practicing various

PEARLS OF WISDOM

"Cash Is King."

Be sure your financial house is in order before you risk money on stocks. Start by paying off as much debt as possible, considering that your **credit cards** probably cost you anywhere between 12 and 20 percent in interest. You'd have to make an equivalent return on your investments just to break even, which is possible but perhaps difficult to maintain on a consistent basis.

Next, make sure you have some **cash** ready in a bank account or money market fund in case you run into trouble somewhere along the way. Many experts recommend that you have access to at least three month's gross wages in case you lose your job.

investment strategies, learning about companies and their financials, and keeping abreast of news and happenings that affect the economy and the companies, anyone can become adept enough to do well in the stock market. But just as some people can pick up an instrument and develop an extraordinary ability to play it in short order (while most other people will struggle to develop even a basic level of skill), some people possess gifts or talents for investing that will manifest themselves in extraordinarily successful track records.

Invest in What You Love, the Money Will Follow

A final strategy that can help you develop and strengthen your own intuition for investing is that recommended by Peter Lynch in just about all of his books. The idea is simple and quite effective and involves nothing more than looking around as you carry out your daily life for companies that you know and trust. According to Lynch, if more people considered the companies they did business with as potential investment opportunities, many more successful investors would be among us. How does this technique help to develop intuition? Primarily by developing your awareness for what makes a business successful and profitable. If, for example, you tend to shop in a certain discount store, you may want to take note when you visit of whether that store is frequently packed with customers or if you are the only one in there. A crowded store is a great sign because it indicates strong sales, which can mean positive earnings and cash flow for a company. You still need to research the company before you invest to make sure it is being managed competently and has positive earnings and little debt. You may also want to take

note of the current economic trends in your area or in the country as a whole. If people show a growing tendency to shop at discount stores because of economic conditions that make it necessary to save money, you may have discovered a great investment opportunity just by going shopping on a Saturday afternoon. The knack is learning to see the big picture and how the company you are considering fits into this picture. Over time, you'll develop the perception that will help you make the right decisions and become a more successful investor.

In the final analysis, success in stocks is a combination of art and science and intuition. You shouldn't invest in a company solely on the basis of a momentary gut feeling or flash of inspiration. But if you have such an experience, don't necessarily throw it out the window as irrelevant and useless, either. Sometimes your hunches can be exceptional leads, but you've got to take that intuitive sense and dig in a little with your science (by finding out about the company and its fundamentals) and your art (by assimilating information from other sources that may relate to your potential investment and determining how that information might affect your investment). There's no such thing as a sure thing, but if you develop your knowledge so you know what information is really important and your ability to recognize good opportunities when they come along, you stand a better than average chance of achieving success in the stock market.

WRAP *it* up, *set some* GOALS!

CHAPTER TEN

Now that you have a good understanding of how the **stock market works,** you need to do some hard and fast thinking in order to pick your investment **goals.**

Setting goals can be as easy as asking yourself these two primary questions:

1. How much do I need to gain?

2. How much can I afford to lose?

Setting clear guidelines for yourself in these two areas will not only help you time your purchases and sales of stock more consistently, but will also help you sleep more soundly at night. No one likes to think about losing money in the markets, but we all know of people who have lost money in stocks. Listening to people talk about the

markets after they've taken a financial hit is like listening to someone talk about World War II. It's enough to scare away even the most adventurous investors. But while losing money is certainly unpleasant, it is a possibility that must be faced. If you've prepared yourself to deal with loss in a constructive way, you'll be able to handle it much more effectively.

Start by setting a desired goal for your investment returns. Do you want to outperform the S&P 500 average? The Dow Jones Average? The Russell 2000? If you consider the history of the stock market since 1930, you'll see that the average annual return for the S&P 500, for example, has been 11 percent. The Dow Jones Average has followed suit with a similar average return. If your goal is to equal the performance of the S&P 500, you might just as well avoid the effort of picking your own stocks and purchase shares of the Vanguard Index Trust 500 mutual fund. As you saw in Chapter Seven, this fund's sole purpose is to equal the returns of the S&P 500 index by investing in all of the stocks in that index. If your desire is to outperform the averages, you'll either have to be lucky enough to find a mutual fund that can consistently provide stellar results, or you'll have to do your own legwork and pick good stocks using some of the strategies mentioned in Chapter Six.

If you decide that you want 20 percent returns on each of your stocks, you'll have a yardstick in hand by which to measure your investing record. If you bought Zza stock at $10 and sold it at $12, you've met your goal. Congratulations! But when you set goals, it is very important that you learn to live with the results of the decisions prompted by those goals. If you see Zza climb to $15 per share in the months after you sold it, don't give yourself a hard time about the money you "lost" by not holding on longer. The fact is that your 20 percent return is far better than many investors ever experience on their stocks, and you should be pleased with your outstanding performance. There's nothing to be gained by kicking yourself later if the stock goes higher. Investing is about making money, and your 20 percent return certainly made good money for you.

How does anyone ever double an investment if they always sell at 20 percent? This is where the art of investing comes into play. If your stock has increased to the point at which you've made a 20 percent return, instead of selling it outright, you may want to reevaluate the stock to see if the fundamentals are still strong. Ask yourself if you'd still be willing to buy Zza at $12. If the answer, based on your research and analysis of the company's prospects, is a resounding and unequivocal "Yes!" then hang on. You may be in for an exciting ride into what Peter Lynch calls a "ten-bagger." That's his technical term for a stock that increases tenfold in value. A ten-bagger is far better than 20 percent, but not all stocks are going to produce those results. Setting clear goals can help you determine milestones for when to reevaluate your stocks. If you've made your 20 percent and the fundamentals don't excite you anymore, go ahead and sell. You've done well, so don't fret if the price goes up another dollar or two.

The next step is to consider the downside of investing. William O'Neil, in *How to Make Money in Stocks,* suggests that an investor should set a loss limit of about 10 percent. Using this strategy, if Zza drops from $10 to $9, you'll consider selling. You may not want to dump the stock automatically when a certain number is hit. Instead, you should reconsider the reasons you bought the stock in the first place and see if those reasons still apply. If the fundamentals still look good to you and you still think you'd buy the stock at the current price, you may want to hold on and see if the stock rises again. If you really feel good about the company's prospects, you may even want to buy more of the stock.

While averaging down your price like this can be risky (why throw good money after bad?), if you still think the stock is strong for the long term, why not take advantage of an opportunity to get more at a better price? Setting a clear goal for limiting your losses is wise and will keep you from being surprised by a steadily dropping price, but you have to use your wisdom to consider each and every investment you make individually. As you've seen in the case of Zza, if you took your losses at $9, you'd have missed out on a great long-term opportunity.

Consistency and Regular Investing

One area of weakness for many investors is consistency. Unfortunately, most inexperienced investors tend to buy when the market or a stock is at its highest and sell when things look bleak. This strategy works great for consistently losing a great deal of money. One of the best ways to profit in stocks is to invest regularly over a long period of time. If you're smart with your stock selections and research the companies whose stock you want to buy, you can profit even during bear markets or general eco-

nomic setbacks. If you read Michael O'Higgins' book, *Beating the Dow,* you'll see that his basic method has performed exceedingly well historically, even during the period of 1972–1974, one of the worst bear markets in history. The key is to invest consistently in good companies and not let yourself be scared out of the market if things take a negative turn.

Another area in which consistency can pay off with great returns is in mutual fund investing. Compounded income on reinvested dividends or gains can produce marvelous results over the course of a few years. In fact, Einstein himself is said to have marveled at the miraculous long-term effects of compounding. Why is compounding such a tremendous opportunity for patient investors? Consider that you've just put $1,000 into Zedley's Ten Percent Fund (ZTPF), a stock mutual fund that guarantees a 10 percent annually compounded return. Next year at this time, you'll have $1,100 in the fund. But the following year, you won't have $1,200 but rather $1,210, because the fund will have paid you 10 percent that second year not on $1,000 but on $1,100. While this extra $10 may not seem like much initially, keep in mind that if you're consistently adding to your investment over time, the amount of money available to produce that 10 percent return will continue to grow fantastically. This simple example shows the effect of annual compounding, but many investments compound (or calculate) interest on a quarterly, monthly, weekly, or even daily basis. The shorter the compounding period, the greater the effect. But you've got to be consistent over a long period of time to realize the benefits of compounding. Time can actually be your best friend if you allow it the opportunity to work for you.

Listen to Everyone, Think for Yourself

As a final piece of advice, remember that you alone are ultimately responsible for your investments and your financial well-being. Learning as much as you can about investing and stocks and businesses and companies is certainly important, because you're very unlikely to become a successful investor without the appropriate knowledge. It's also important to talk to other investors and brokers to learn from their experiences. You can get advice and information from people who have been there before you, and the wisdom of someone who's already traveled to these places is truly worth a great deal. But in the end, you are the one who is (and should be) responsible for the performance of your own investment portfolio. When you make that decision to buy or

sell a stock, be sure you are confident and clear about your reasons, and if you suffer a loss, don't get discouraged. Rather, analyze your mistakes to see what you can learn from them. And when you make a nice profit on your carefully considered and wisely chosen investments, go ahead and pat yourself on the back. You deserve it.

GLOSSARY

accounts payable: Money that a company owes.

accounts receivable: Money that a company has not yet received from its customers for the sale of goods or services.

accrued expense: An expense incurred that has not yet been paid.

accumulated depreciation: The total amount that an asset has lost in value since it was acquired.

advisor: A company that, or individual who, for a fee manages the portfolios of investors.

aggressive growth stock: Stock in a company that is small but rapidly expanding, which gives the investor the opportunity to attain above average returns.

American Stock Exchange (AMEX): The second largest stock exchange in the United States.

AMEX Market Value Index: A measurement of all the stocks on the American Stock Exchange.

analyst: A person who works for brokerages, insurance companies, banks, mutual funds, or other investment businesses who studies the market and produces reports on stocks and particular industries.

annual meeting of shareholders: The gathering once a year of shareholders of a corporation to elect directors, discuss the financial state of the company, and vote on resolutions.

annual report: A document presented to stockholders once a year that includes information about how the company is doing. It contains the balance sheet, income statement, and statement of cash flows as well as discussions about the business.

appreciate: To increase in value.

asking price: The price an investor pays to purchase a stock.

asset: Something of value (e.g., inventory, equipment, or real estate).

at the money: The condition of an option when its underlying stock reaches the strike price before its expiration date.

average: A measurement used to determine the value of sectors of the stock market and the market as a whole. The Dow Jones Industrial Average is one example.

averaging down: A strategy whereby an investor buys additional stock at a lower price than the original purchase price in the hope that the stock price will increase.

balance sheet: A financial document that includes a company's assets and liabilities and the owners's equity.

bankruptcy: The condition in which corporations or individuals legally declare that they cannot meet their financial obligations.

bear market: A prolonged period of falling stock prices. Opposite of a bull market.

bid price: The price an investor receives for the sale of a stock.

blue chip stock: The stock of a large, relatively stable, well-established company. The name comes from the blue chips in a poker game, the chips with the highest value.

board of directors: A group of individuals responsible for managing the affairs of a corporation.

bond: An interest-bearing debt instrument.

book value: The amount of cash that a company could expect to generate if it were to liquidate.

broker: A company that, or an individual who, facilitates a stock transaction but does not own the stock at the end of the sale.

broker/dealer: A special class of brokerage firm that places buy and sell orders for clients and also sells stock that it keeps in its own inventory.

bull market: A prolonged period of rising stock prices. Opposite of a bear market.

business sales and inventories index: Measurements of the sum of sales in manufacturing, retail, and wholesale trade for a specified period, and the amount of goods held by businesses in inventory that have yet to be sold.

Buttonwood Agreement: The contract drawn by 24 brokers in 1792 to trade securities that marked the establishment of the New York Stock Exchange.

buy-and-hold: A strategy whereby an investor purchases securities and holds on to them, taking into consideration the long-term outlook of the underlying companies.

call: An option to buy an asset at a fixed price until a specific date.

C-A-N S-L-I-M: An investment strategy created by William J. O'Neil that analyzes seven aspects of a stock: current earnings, annual earnings, new developments, supply and demand, industry leader, institutional investor support, and market direction.

capital gain: Money an investor earns by selling a stock for a profit.

capitalism: An economic system based on private ownership of corporations.

capital loss: Money an investor loses by selling a stock for less than the price paid for it.

cash flow: A measurement of a company's cash receipts and disbursements over a given period of time.

chart: A graph that shows a stock's price and volume of trading over a period of time.

churning: The practice whereby a broker advises a client to buy and sell in quick succession for no apparent reason other than to earn the broker additional commissions.

close an option position: To buy an option and sell it back to make a profit.

closing price: The price at which a stock trades at the end of a trading session.

commission: The fee charged by a broker to negotiate the purchase or sale of a security.

commodity: Raw materials like metals, grains, or minerals that can be processed and resold.

common stock: A type of stock that entitles the holder to have voting rights in the corporation and a claim to what remains after all the creditors and preferred stockholders have been paid, if the company goes out of business.

compound interest: Interest that is earned on both the principal and the interest on that principal.

Consumer Price Index (CPI): An index that measures the changes in price of a group of goods and services purchased by all wage-earning consumers.

corporation: A form of business that is registered with the state and considered an independent entity with legal rights and responsibilities separate from the individuals who own it.

correction: A drop in the overall value of stock prices in a market that was climbing steadily. The decline brings the prices down to a more reasonable level.

covered option: An option that is written by an investor who owns shares of the underlying stock.

crash: An unusually large drop in the overall value of stock prices on a particular day.

credit line: A credit arrangement whereby a lending institution agrees to lend a borrower a certain amount over a specified period of time.

creditor: An individual or institution to whom money is owed.

currency risk: The danger that fluctuations in currency values will affect investments, particularly for investors in international stocks.

day trader: An investor who makes buy and sell decisions based on small, short-term stock price fluctuations.

dealer: An individual who facilitates stock transactions and makes a profit by selling the stock for a higher price than that which was paid for it.

deep-discount broker: A broker who offers almost no services or advice, but who facilitates trades for a greatly reduced commission.

deflation: The rate at which the real cost of goods and services declines in the economy.

depreciation: Loss of value.

derivative: A hybrid security, the value of which is based on another security. Options and futures are examples of derivatives.

digest of earnings report: A report found in the financial press that contains information about a company's quarterly earnings statement, including revenues, net income, number of shares outstanding, and earnings per share for the current quarter and the same quarter of the previous year.

dilution: The decrease in value of a stock caused by an increase in the number of shares outstanding.

disclosure statement: The document required by the SEC when a company has an initial public offering (IPO). It includes a statement of business purpose, how management intends to grow the business, the number of shares of stock the company is issuing, and what management intends to do with the money earned from the IPO.

discount broker: A broker who facilitates trades for a reduced commission without offering services and information.

disposable income: Income that can be spent for non-necessary purchases as well as necessities.

diversification: An investment strategy that relies on distributing investments among a variety of securities to minimize risk.

dividend: A payment issued by a company that distributes part of its profits and earnings to shareholders.

Dividend Reinvestment Programs (DRIPs): Programs offered by many large companies that enable investors to purchase stock directly without brokers.

dividend stock: A stock that is expected to pay out dividends on a regular basis.

dividend yield: The amount an investment will earn calculated by dividing the annual dividend by the current price of the stock.

dollar cost averaging: An investment strategy whereby an investor contributes equal amounts of money to an investment at regular intervals.

Dow Jones Averages: Measurements of the stock prices of industrial, transportation, and utility stocks. The indexes are used as gauges to determine general attitudes toward the different sectors of the market.

Dow Jones Industrial Average (DJIA): The oldest and most widely followed index, the DJIA measures the stock of 30 large, successful U.S. industrial companies. It is used to gauge the overall strength and weakness of the American economy.

Dow Jones Transportation Average: An index that measures the stock prices of 20 railroads, airlines, and trucking companies.

Dow Jones Utility Average: An index that measures the stock prices of 15 large gas, oil, electric, and other energy companies.

earnings: The income of a business.

earnings per share (EPS): A measure of a company's profitability calculated by dividing net income by shares outstanding on the income statement.

economic risk: The danger to investors that the economy will decline.

exchange rate: The price of one currency as it relates to the price of another currency.

exercise an option: To buy or sell the underlying stock of an option.

expansion: The period of an economic cycle during which the economy grows beyond the level of the last peak.

expense ratio: A line on an income statement calculated by dividing the expenses by the revenues.

Federal Reserve System: An independent bank that governs the U.S. money supply.

Federal Trade Commission (FTC): A U.S. government agency that regulates competitive markets with regard to discouraging monopolies and encouraging free trade.

FIFO (First-In/First-Out): A formula for calculating capital gains or losses based on which transaction occurred first.

financial planner: A person who provides advice about identifying financial goals and developing strategies for meeting them.

Foolish Four: An investment strategy created by David and Tom Gardner that combines the five highest-yielding, lowest-priced Dow stocks with the second lowest-priced of the highest-yielding stocks.

fraud: Deception for personal gain by the means of false statements or actions.

full disclosure statement: A document required by the Securities and Exchange Commission that corporations must file before the initial public offering of a stock. It includes financial data, background of the company's officers, a description of what the firm intends to do with the money raised from the sale of the stock, and other information. [See: disclosure statement.]

full-service broker: A stockbroker who provides services and information to clients in addition to facilitating trades.

fundamental analysis: An investment strategy that relies on evaluating a stock based on the company's historical growth and profit patterns.

fundamentals: A company's underlying financial situation.

futures contract: An agreement to take delivery or deliver a specific commodity (e.g., grains, metals, or foreign currencies) on a particular date.

going public: The process by which a corporation offers stock to the public.

Great Depression: A period of economic decline that started with the stock market crash of 1929 and lasted through the 1930s.

Gross Domestic Product (GDP): A measurement of the total production of goods and services in the United States during a specified period of time.

growth stock: A stock that has the potential of increasing in price as the company expands and prospers.

hedging: An investment strategy that reduces risk on a stock that is already owned. An example of hedging is when an investor buys a put option to help offset any losses from the stock she owns.

housing starts: A measurement of the number of homes that are beginning to be built during a specified period.

income statement: A financial document that includes the expenses, revenues, and net income of a business. Also known as a profit and loss (P&L) statement.

income stock: A stock that tends to pay regular dividends but which may not appreciate significantly in value.

incorporate: To undergo a process in which a business becomes registered with the state and is considered an independent entity with legal rights and responsibilities separate from the individuals who own it.

index: A measurement of the performance of a stock market. Standard & Poor's 500 is an example of an index.

index fund: A mutual fund that invests in all the stocks of companies in a particular index.

index option: An option with a stock index as its underlying asset.

inflation: The rate at which the real cost of goods and services rises in the economy.

initial public offering (IPO): A first-time offering of stock for sale to the general public.

insider trading: The illegal manipulation of the stock market, with the intent of profiting from that manipulation, by employees and/or officers of a corporation through the use of information not available to the general public.

institutional investor: A company like a mutual fund or pension fund that invests on the behalf of many individuals.

intangible asset: An asset with no physical properties.

interest: Payment for money that is borrowed.

in the money: 1) The condition that exists for a call option when the price of its underlying stock goes higher than the strike price. 2) The condition that exists for a put option when the price of the underlying stock is less than the strike price move.

intrinsic value: The value of a stock based on financial data.

inventory: Raw materials and finished goods a company intends to sell.

investment banker: Also known as an underwriter, an investment banker buys stock directly from corporations that are going public and attempts to resell the stock to investors.

investment objective: What an individual or mutual fund expects to gain from investing. Examples of investment objectives are capital gains or steady dividend income.

investor: Someone who gives money for the purpose of financial gain.

large-capitalization stock: A stock of a big company.

leading economic indicators: Measurements of business and consumer activity.

liability: An obligation to pay a certain amount to another party.

lien: A creditor's legal right to sell the mortgaged assets of a debtor when the debtor fails to meet loan payments.

liquidate: To convert assets into cash.

liquidity: The characteristic of an asset that allows it to be converted to cash.

majority shareholder: A shareholder who has at least 51 percent of the stock in a corporation.

manager risk: The danger to mutual fund investors that the manager of the fund is incompetent or makes unwise decisions.

manipulate: To cause a stock to sell at an artificial price by buying and selling it inappropriately.

margin account: A brokerage account that permits clients to purchase stock on credit and to borrow against securities in the account.

margin call: A broker's demand that an investor deposit additional cash or securities in his account, usually because the securities the investor bought on margin decreased to a certain level or the total value of the equity in his account drops below a certain level.

market capitalization: The total value of a company's outstanding shares calculated by multiplying the total number of shares outstanding by the price per share.

market maker: A dealer who maintains an inventory of stocks.

market risk: The danger that the stock market as a whole will decline.

market timing: The ability to predict when stock prices are going to start to rise or decline.

mid-cap stock: A stock of a medium-sized company.

money market: Short-term, low-risk nonequity securities such as commercial paper, Treasury bills, and certificates of deposit.

municipal bond: Debt security issued by cities that is free from federal taxes and may be exempt from state taxes if the purchaser lives in the state in which the issuing municipality is located.

mutual fund: An investment company that pools the resources of hundreds or thousands of individuals to enable them to diversify in a variety of investments, including stocks, bonds, and money markets.

naked option: An option that is written on stock that the investor does not own.

Nasdaq OTC Composite Index: A measurement of the stock prices of over-the-counter stocks.

Nasdaq Stock Market (National Association of Securities Dealers Automated Quotation System): An electronic, screen-based equity market operated and regulated by the National Association of Securities Dealers (NASD).

National Association of Securities Dealers (NASD): The self-regulatory organization of brokers and dealers responsible for the operation of the Nasdaq Stock Market and the regulation of the over-the-counter market.

net change: The difference between the closing price of the current session and the closing price of the previous trading session.

net income: Income after all taxes and expenses have been subtracted.

newsgroup: An Internet electronic bulletin board that allows participants to post messages and respond to each other.

New York Stock Exchange (NYSE): The largest and most active stock market in the world, the NYSE mostly trades stock of large companies.

NYSE Composite Index: The most frequently consulted NYSE index, the NYSE Composite Index measures all the common stocks listed on the NYSE.

odd lot: Blocks of stock up to 99 shares.

option: A contract to buy or sell an asset (e.g., shares of a stock) at a set price until a specific date. [See put and call.]

optional dividend: A dividend payout that can be taken in shares of stock instead of in cash.

out of the money: The condition that exists for options whose underlying stocks are below the strike price (for calls) or above the strike price (for puts).

over-the-counter (OTC): Securities trading via computer, telephone, or direct negotiations rather than at a physical location. OTC stocks are generally of newer, less established companies.

paper gain/loss: A gain or loss experienced by an investor when the price of a stock increases above or declines below the price at which it was purchased. If the investor doesn't sell the stock, the gain or loss is unrealized.

peak: The point in an economic cycle at which the economy is strongest.

penny stock: A speculative stock that sells for $1 or less.

pension fund: An institution that invests, controls, and disburses money to retirees.

Penultimate Profit Prospect (PPP): An investment strategy created by Michael O'Higgins that recommends purchasing the second lowest-priced stock from among the ten highest-yielding stocks of the Dow Jones Industrial Average.

pink sheets: Daily pricing information for OTC stocks.

portfolio: A group of investments.

preferred stock: A type of stock that gives the stockholder first dibs over common stockholders to the assets and dividends of the company if the company goes out of business. Preferred stockholders are guaranteed fixed dividends but have no voting rights.

premium: The price of an option.

price-to-book ratio: A measure of a company's value calculated by dividing the share price by the book value per share.

price-to-earnings (PE) ratio: The most common measure of a stock's value calculated by dividing the current share price by the earnings per share.

price-to-sales ratio (PSR): A method of measuring a stock's value calculated by dividing the company's market capitalization by the previous year's total revenues.

prime rate: A general indicator of the direction of interest rates. A benchmark to which other rates are pegged.

principal: The original sum of money invested.

privately held corporation: A corporation that does not sell its stock to the public.

private placement: The sale of securities without a public offering.

profit: Income that is left after expenses have been deducted.

profit and loss (P&L) statement: [See income statement.]

profit margin: The line on an income statement derived by dividing the net income by the revenue.

prospectus: The document a company prepares and uses to sell stock when it is undertaking an IPO. It includes financial data, a business plan, description of the firm's officers, and mention of any pending lawsuits. The prospectus is a shortened version of the disclosure statement submitted to the SEC.

proxy: Absentee ballot for shareholders to vote at an annual meeting.

publicly held corporation: A corporation that sells its stock to the public.

put: An option to sell an asset at a fixed price until a specific date.

quarter: Three-month period.

quote: The price at which a stock trades.

recession: The period in an economic cycle during which business activity and spending are declining.

recovery: The period in an economic cycle during which businesses regain losses.

registered representative: A stockbroker who has successfully passed the NASD's registration process.

research and development (R&D): The process of developing and bringing new products to market or improving existing products.

resistance: A theoretical upper limit that seems to stop the price of a stock from rising further.

retail sales measurement: A monthly measurement of total retail sales, in dollars, gathered from a voluntary survey of thousands of U.S. retail businesses.

retained earnings: Money a company has earned from sales that it reinvests into the business before paying dividends.

revenue: The intake of assets in the form of dividends, interest, rent, and the sale of goods and services.

reverse split: A process by which the number of shares of a company's stock decreases while the price of the stock increases.

risk: The uncertainty of investment returns.

round lot: A block of 100 shares of stock.

Russell 2000: An index that tracks the stock prices of 2,000 small-capitalization companies whose average market capitalization is $288 million.

seat: Membership on a securities exchange that enables one to trade securities directly without a broker.

sector: A group of securities in the same market category.

Securities Act of 1933: Legislation that sought to protect small investors from fraud, regulate the stock market, and prevent market crashes.

Securities and Exchange Commission (SEC): The federal regulatory agency that oversees the securities markets and administers the securities laws.

security: A stock, bond, or option that represents ownership in a corporation or a loan to a corporation or government.

share: A single unit of ownership in a corporation or mutual fund.

shareholder: A person who owns stock in a corporation or mutual fund.

shareholders's equity: The value of stock outstanding.

shorting: A method of investing in which a profit is made from a stock if it decreases in value by having a broker borrow shares from another investor, sell the shares, and then deposit the proceeds into his customer's account. If the price of the stock drops below the price the customer paid for it, the broker buys the same number of shares, returns them to the lender, and gives the customer the difference.

short squeeze: A condition of a short position in which a large number of people close their positions, driving up the stock price.

small-capitalization stock: The stock of a relatively small company. Because the performance of this type of company is unpredictable, the stock is subject to large price fluctuations—a good deal of risk is involved, but an investor has the potential to realize a big capital gain.

specialist: A broker's broker, who maintains an inventory of stocks and ensures that a buyer can find a seller and a seller can find a buyer.

speculation: The practice of purchasing any investment based on its potential selling price instead of its actual value.

split: A process by which the number of shares of outstanding stock in a company increases but the price of the stock decreases.

spread: The difference in cost between a stock's bid price and asking price.

Standard & Poor's 500 Stock Index (S&P 500): A measurement of the stock prices of 500 small-cap, mid-cap, and large-capitalization companies in a variety of sectors that uses a weighted calculating system (stock price times shares outstanding). Thus larger-capitalization companies influence the index more than lower-capitalization companies.

statement of cash flows: A financial document that provides information about specific inflows and outflows of cash that a company has experienced over a certain period of time.

stock: A share of ownership in a corporation.

stock market: A place where people buy and sell shares of corporate ownership.

street name: A description of the process whereby a broker keeps shares in an account set aside for a particular investor.

strike price: The price at which an investor can exercise her option, if the price is reached before the expiration date.

supply and demand: A law of economics that says that if something is in little supply but in great demand, the price of the item will rise.

support: A theoretical bottom-level price below which a stock will not drop.

symbol: A one-letter to five-letter abbreviation assigned to a stock.

syndicate: A group of investment banking firms.

technical analysis: An investment strategy that uses the historical patterns of a stock's price movement to predict future prices.

ten-bagger: A stock that increases tenfold in value.

10-K statement: A detailed analysis of a company's financial condition filed annually with the Securities and Exchange Commission.

10-Q statement: A company's financial report, less detailed than the 10-K, filed quarterly with the Securities and Exchange Commission.

tombstone: A public notice of an initial public offering (IPO).

trader: A dealer who buys and sells stock independently of customer orders.

trading: Buying and selling securities.

trading volume: The amount of trading of a security or a market.

triple-witching days: The days on which stock options, stock index options, and stock index futures expire simultaneously (the third Friday of every March, June, September, and December).

trough: The lowest point of an economic cycle.

undervalued stock: A stock that trades at a price lower than it should, based on its financial data.

underwriter: [See investment banker.]

unemployment rate: A measurement of the rate of unemployment during a speci-fied time period.

U.S. Treasury bill: A short-term debt security of the U.S. Treasury.

U.S. Treasury bond: A longer-term debt security of the U.S. Treasury.

U.S. Treasury note: An intermediate-term debt security of the U.S. Treasury.

value investing: An investment technique that relies on an examination of the under-lying value of a corporation as the primary criterion for deciding whether or not to buy the company's stock.

Value Line Investment Survey: A report that ranks the stocks of over 1,000 com-panies on the basis of industry ranking, timeliness, safety, and other measures. It also provides information about historical pricing and trading volume, as well as a stock analyst's evaluation of each stock.

Vanguard Index Trust 500: A mutual fund that purchases stock of every company listed in the S&P 500 index.

venture capitalist: An individual or firm that invests in typically small, young companies.

volatility: A stock's price swings.

volume: The number of shares traded.

Wall Street: The main street of New York City's financial district. It has become syn-onymous with investments and finance.

Wilshire 5000 Equity Index: An index that measures the performance of all equity securities headquartered in the United States.

yield: A figure on a stock table that is calculated by dividing the dividend amount by the current price, then multiplying by 100.

RESOURCES

Books

Beating the Street. Peter Lynch, with John Rothchild (Fireside, 1994).

Directory of Corporate Affiliations. (National Register Publishing, updated annually).

Everyone's Money Book, 3rd Edition. Jordan Goodman (Dearborn Trade, 2001).

How to Buy Stocks the Smart Way. Stephen Littauer (Dearborn Financial Publishing, 1995).

Learn to Earn: A Beginner's Guide to the Basics of Investing and Business. Peter Lynch, with John Rothchild (Fireside, 1996).

The Motley Fool Investment Guide. David and Tom Gardner (Fireside, 1997).

One Up on Wall Street: How to Use What You Already Know to Make Money in the Market. Peter Lynch, with John Rothchild (Simon & Schuster, 2000).

Online Trading Survival Guide. Jack Guinan (Dearborn Trade, 2000).

The 100 Best Stocks to Own in America, 6th Edition. Gene Walden (Dearborn Financial Publishing, 1999).

The Savage Truth on Money. Terry Savage (John Wiley & Sons, 1999).

Stocks for the Long Run. Jeremy Siegel and Peter Bernstein (McGraw-Hill, 1998).

Wall Street Picks for 2000. Kirk Kazanjian (Dearborn Financial Publishing, 1999).

Magazines and Newspapers

Barron's. 200 Liberty Street, New York, NY 10281, 800-568-7625, $145/yr., weekly. <www.barons.com>

Bloomberg Personal Finance. 499 Park Avenue, New York, NY 10022, $14.95/yr., monthly. <www.bloomberg.com>

BusinessWeek. 1221 Avenue of the Americas, New York, NY 10020, 800-635-1200, $49.95/yr., weekly (51 issues). <www.businessweek.com>

Fast Company. 77 North Washington Street, Boston, MA 02114-1927, 800-542-6029, $23.95/yr., monthly. <www.fastcompany.com>

Forbes. 60 Fifth Avenue, New York, NY 10011, 800-888-9896, $59.95/yr., biweekly. <www.forbes.com>

Fortune. Time & Life Building, Rockefeller Center, New York, NY 10020-1393, 800-621-8000, $59.95/yr., biweekly. <www.fortune.com>

Inc. PO Box 54129, Boulder, CO 80332, 800-234-0999, $14/yr. (18 issues). <www.inc.com>

Individual Investor. PO Box 37289, Boone, IA 50037-0289, 888-616-7677, $19.95/yr., monthly. <www.individualinvestor.com>

Investor's Business Daily. 12655 Beatrice Street, Los Angeles, CA 90066, 800-831-2525, $197/yr., daily. <www.investors.com>

Kiplinger's Personal Finance. 1729 H Street, NW, Washington, DC 20006, 800-544-0155, $19.95/yr., monthly. <www.kiplinger.com>

Money. PO Box 60001, Tampa, FL 33660-0001, $39.89/yr. (13 issues). <www.money.com>

The New York Times. PO Box 2047, South Hackensack, NJ 07606, 800-631-2500, $374.40/yr., daily. <www.nytimes.com>

Smart Money. PO Box 7538, Red Oak, IA 51591, 800-444-4204, $24/yr., monthly.

The Wall Street Journal. 84 Second Avenue, Chicopee, MA 01020, 800-568-7625, $175/yr., five days per week delivery. <www.wsj.com>

Worth. 650 Fifth Avenue, New York, NY 10019 800-777-1851, $12/yr. (10 issues). <www.worth.com>

Newsletters and Reports

Standard & Poor's Stock Reports. 25 Broadway, New York, NY 10004, 800-221-5277, $145/yr., monthly. (stock guide)
<www.stockinfo.standardpoor.com>

Stockmarket Cycles. PO Box 6873, Santa Rosa, CA 95406, 707-769-4800.
<www.stockmarketcycles.com>

The Value Line Investment Survey. PO Box 3988, New York, NY 10008, 800-833-0046, $570/yr., weekly. <www.valueline.com>

Zacks Analyst Watch. Zacks Investment Research, Inc., 155 North Wacker Drive, Chicago, IL 60606, 800-399-6659, $295/yr., monthly.
<www.zacks.com>

Online Resources

American Stock Exchange <www.amex.com>

Bloomberg <www.bloomberg.com>

BusinessWeek Online <www.businessweek.com>

Chicago Board of Trade <www.cbot.com>

Chicago Mercantile Exchange <www.cme.com>

Chicago Stock Exchange <www.chicagostockex.com>

Doug Gerlach's Invest-O-Rama <www.investorama.com>

EDGAR <www.edgar-online.com>

E*TRADE <www.etrade.com>

Federal Trade Commission <www.ftc.gov>

Fidelity <www.fid-inv.com>

Financenter <www.financenter.com>

FTSE International <www.ftse.com>

Goldman Sachs <www.gs.com>

Hoover's Online <www.hoovers.com>

Internal Revenue Service <www.irs.ustreas.gov>

Investor's Edge < www.investorsedge.cibc.com >

Lebenthal < www.lebenthal.com >

Legg Mason < www.leggmason.com >

London Stock Exchange AIM (Alternative Investment Market)
< www.stockex.co.uk/aim >

Merrill Lynch < www.ml.com >

Morgan Stanley Dean Witter < www.msdw.com >

Motley Fool < www.fool.com >

Nasdaq Stock Market < www.nasdaq.com >

NETworth < www.quicken.com/investments >

New York Mercantile Exchange < www.nymex.com >

New York Stock Exchange < www.nyse.com >

New York Times Online < www.nyt.com >

Philadelphia Stock Exchange < www.phlx.com >

Piper Jaffray < www.piperjaffray.com >

Prudential Securities < www.prusec.com >

Quicken Financial Network < www.quicken.com >

Quote.com < www.quote.com >

Salomon Smith Barney < www.smithbarney.com >

Schwab < www.schwab.com >

Securities and Exchange Commission < www.sec.gov >

Silicon Investor < www.techstocks.com >

Stein Roe < www.steinroe.com >

Stock Smart < www.stocksmart.com >

T. Rowe Price < www.troweprice.com >

Tokyo Stock Exchange < www.tse.or.jp >

Vanguard < www.vanguard.com >

Worth < www.worth.com >

Investment Clubs

National Association of Investors Corporation. 711 West Thirteen Mile Road, Madison Heights, MI 48071, 248-583-6242. For listings of local investment clubs in your area. <www.better-investing.org>

Associations and Organizations

American Association of Individual Investors. 625 North Michigan Avenue, Suite 1900, Chicago, IL 60611, 312-280-0170, 800-428-2244. <www.aaii.org>

American Stock Exchange. 86 Trinity Place, New York, NY 10006, 212-306-1000. <www.amex.com>

Dun & Bradstreet. 8310 Capital of Texas Highway N, Austin, TX 78731, 800-234-3867. <www.dnb.com>

Investment Company Institute. 1401 H Street, NW, Suite 1200, Washington, DC 20005, 202-326-5800. <www.ici.org>

National Association of Investors Corporation. 711 West Thirteen Mile Road, Madison Heights, MI 48071, 248-583-6242. <www.better-investing.org>

National Association of Securities Dealers. 1818 N Street, NW, Washington, DC 20036, 800-289-9999. <www.nasdr.com>

National Center for Financial Education. PO Box 34070, San Diego, CA 92163, 619-232-8811. <www.ncfe.org>

National Fraud Information Center. PO Box 65868, Washington, DC 20035, 800-876-7060. <www.fraud.org>

New York Stock Exchange. 11 Wall Street, New York, NY 10005, 212-656-3000. <www.nyse.com>

North American Securities Administrators Association. 10 G Street NE, Suite 710, Washington, DC 20002, 202-737-0900. <www.nasaa.com>

Securities and Exchange Commission. Office of Investor Education & Assistance. 450 Fifth Street, NW, Washington, DC 20549, 202-942-7040. <www.sec.gov>

INDEX